The Art of Middle Management in Secondary Schools

A Guide to Effective Subject and Team Leadership

Peter Fleming

David Fulton Publishers

London

David Fulton Publishers Ltd
Ormond House, 26–27 Boswell Street, London WC1N 3JD

First published in Great Britain by David Fulton Publishers 2000

Note: The right of Peter Fleming to be identified as the author of this work has been asserted by him in accordance with the Copyright, Designs and Patents Act 1988.

Copyright © Peter Fleming 2000

British Library Cataloguing in Publication Data
A catalogue record for this book is available from the British Library

ISBN 1–85346–623–9

Typeset by Elite Typesetting Techniques, Eastleigh, Hampshire
Printed in Great Britain by The Cromwell Press Ltd, Trowbridge, Wilts.

Contents

Preface

As we begin the new millennium, schools face the challenge of continuing to raise standards of achievement by becoming ever more effective. It is now clear that middle managers have a pivotal role to play in this process. The DfEE and OFSTED alike have highlighted the key contribution effective middle managers can make in creating a 'can do' culture in schools and in ensuring quality practice at classroom level.

The skills required to be an effective middle manager in a secondary school are many and varied but people management skills lie at the heart of getting the best out of both teachers and pupils. Motivating people and building a collaborative team ethos are at the core of effective management. This book is about how middle managers can contribute to raising the quality of education in their schools through proficient team leadership. In 1998 the Teacher Training Agency (TTA) published *National Standards for Subject Leaders*, underlining the importance being placed on middle management in the drive to improve achievement in schools. Generic skills highlighted in this document which are of value to both subject and pastoral team leaders are covered in this book. A summary is provided as an appendix.

Using evidence from a range of sources, case studies and reflection on case studies the book will provide practical advice on:

- what it means to be a manager;
- the importance of vision and ethos;
- how to manage people and build your team;
- how to manage resources and administration;
- how to make meetings and communication effective;
- how to manage change and development;
- how to evaluate the performance of your team;
- how to avoid stress.

The book is intended for three main groups of people, though senior managers in secondary schools, governors and those involved in teacher training and the provision of INSET may also find it useful.

Newly appointed middle managers

For you the book aims to provide clear and practical advice to help you become effective and confident in your role. It will provide guidance on key aspects of middle management facing all team leaders, heads of department, coordinators and year heads. Through the use of case studies it will highlight areas of potential difficulty for managers and in doing so should help you to avoid making major mistakes as you settle into your new post.

Aspiring middle managers

The book should also be of value if you are seeking a middle management post. By introducing you to a range of situations and issues which might form the basis of questions used in the selection process it will help you to prepare for interviews with confidence. It is important to remember that good managers don't have all the answers but they do have a capacity for reflecting clearly on situations and they are able to make rational decisions on the basis of sound judgement. Reflections provided on case studies will help you to think effectively about a range of middle management issues.

Existing middle managers

Successful managers never stop learning and they are continually reviewing their performance. This book grounds comments on effective management in evidence drawn from a range of sources. You will be able to use this evidence to evaluate your approach and consider ways in which you might improve the performance of your team. The emphasis on vision, leadership and creating effective teams will be of particular interest to those who may have underestimated the importance of people skills in the past.

Peter Fleming
Bradford College
November 1999

Acknowledgements

This book would not have been possible without the support of my wife Diane and daughter Rebecca. During its writing they accepted my absence from several family events with good grace. Diane also provided much needed critical feedback on the style and utility of each chapter.

Thanks go to John Owens at David Fulton Publishers for his support, encouragement and useful comments on the early chapters of the book.

I would also like to thank Alan Hall, head teacher of Belle Vue Girls' School, Bradford, for the faith and trust he invested in me during my years as a middle manager in his school. Alan demonstrated that *empowerment* and *collegiality* work, and I feel sure he will recognize much of his philosophy in this book.

The departmental survey (Table 9.2) is reproduced with the kind permission of Paul Hammond, whose web site for heads of department I would strongly recommend (www.hod.org.uk).

CHAPTER ONE

What is Middle Management?

Introduction

When I began teaching in the late 1970s the term 'middle management' was not in widespread use in secondary schools. There were heads of department, year heads and coordinators but people rarely referred to them as *managers*. Indeed, there were heads, deputies and senior teachers but the use of the term *senior management team* (SMT) did not gain widespread usage until well into the 1980s. By contrast, the language of management is now well established in schools and effective school management is seen as a key element in the drive to improve pupil achievement. Training for middle managers now appears regularly on school development plans as this layer of management is seen as pivotal to improving our education system. 'Middle management has the power and responsibility to change systems and reallocate resources to improve "best practice". Relating and cooperating in the pursuit of excellence are basic skills of the middle manager' (Trethowan 1991).

Margaret Thatcher, who wanted to improve efficiency in all areas of the public sector, encouraged this focus on management. It was continued by John Major, whose government admitted to spending £320 million on management consultants, and seems equally popular with Tony Blair. Indeed, before Labour won the general election Mr Blair had sent his entire shadow cabinet to Templeton College, Oxford, to spend a weekend learning about management theory. There is little doubt, therefore, that management has become, and will remain, of central importance in public-sector organizations, including schools.

While there are still some critics of the application of management theory and practice to education it is clear that a good understanding of management as applied to schools is important for any teacher interested in career advancement. More importantly, there is now plenty of evidence to suggest that effective school management is indeed helping to improve standards in schools and for this reason alone an understanding of what constitutes effective middle management is important.

Defining middle management

What, then, do we mean by *middle management*? Managers are people who can use available resources to accomplish a task or reach a target. Middle managers in schools constitute a layer of management between the senior management team and those at the chalk face. They play vital roles in planning for moving a school towards its goals, ensuring the smooth day-to-day operation of school business and monitoring the progress of others. In many schools middle managers provide the 'voice of reason', displaying a clear educational philosophy and idealism but also having their feet firmly on the ground because the bulk of their work is classroom based. Improving the quality of education for young people lies at the heart of school management and being able to motivate and organize individuals and teams to reach goals is essential, as the vast majority of middle management roles involve managing people. In a typical secondary school middle management jobs would include:

Head of Department – Deputy Head of Department – Head of Year – Head of Faculty – Curriculum Coordinator – Exams Officer – Head of Sixth Form – Head of Careers – Head of Resources/Library – Work Experience Coordinator – GNVQ Coordinator – Publicity Officer – SENCO - Key Stage Coordinator

The kind of questions asked at interviews for middle management posts are provided in Table 1.1 and help to clarify the nature of middle management in schools. These questions illustrate that there are four major components to middle management:

- Having a clear vision of the importance of the area you are responsible for and being able to enthuse others with this vision. This is leadership.
- Being clear about what constitutes good practice and using it. This is having specialist knowledge or know-how and being a good practitioner.
- Being an effective manager of people and resources. This involves being able to plan, motivate, encourage good practice, challenge bad practice, solve problems and see tasks through. This is management.
- Being able to put in place procedures to secure efficiency. This is administration.

Successful middle managers usually have, or very quickly develop, specialist knowledge relating to their roles. They then combine

Head of department	*Year head*
What unique learning experiences can your subject bring to young people?	What can a year team contribute to the education of young people?
What teaching strategies would you encourage your colleagues to use?	What qualities does a good form tutor possess?
How would you deal with a member of your team who was regularly experiencing difficulties meeting deadlines?	How would you deal with a tutor who regularly failed to arrive at registration and assembly punctually?
How would you ensure pupil progress was accurately tracked on a modular GCSE course?	How would you ensure effective records of home-school contacts were maintained?

Table 1.1   Interview questions for middle management posts

leadership, management and administration in the right proportions. Less effective middle managers may be good in one area but less effective in others. We can all call to mind heads of department who are good administrators but fail to create any real vision for their team. Equally, heads of department can be very charismatic and inspirational about their subjects but simply fail to put in place systems which result in good day-to-day organization. Some posts will require more of one skill than the others. At certain times the proportion of each skill needed to achieve results may change. Effective middle managers are sensitive to the need to develop their leadership, management and administration skills and are flexible in their application. Good managers are also honest about their weaknesses and will often successfully compensate for them by using the strengths of others in their team. It is reassuring to know that almost all the skills required to be an effective middle manager can be learnt, developed and improved. The art of middle management concerns judgement: the ability to assess a situation and the knack of combining management strategies in just the right proportions are what gives really good middle managers their flair.

The above analysis of middle management is evident in the Teacher Training Agency document *National Standards for Subject Leaders* (1998) which lists the following as key areas of subject leadership:

- strategic direction and development of the subject;
- teaching and learning;

3

- leading and managing staff;
- efficient and effective deployment of staff and resources.

Total quality management (TQM)

Most secondary schools operate a hierarchical model of organization, based on the classical industrial model which is also evident in the armed forces and the Church. This model is best represented as a pyramid with the senior management team at the apex, a layer of middle managers lower down and a broad base of standard scale classroom teachers (see Figure 1.1).

The pyramid is a rigid structure. Roles within it are clearly defined and everyone 'knows their place'. Job descriptions, formal meetings and institutional procedures serve to reinforce the structure. This model tends to hold back individual initiative with people strait-jacketed in their roles and can lead to an 'us and them' mentality. How many times have you heard such questions as 'When are the SMT going to deal with …?' or 'That's for management to sort out – I'm paid to teach'? Most significantly of all, the clients of the school (pupils and parents) are not seen as important.

Management gurus, writing about management in industry and commerce, have argued for almost half a century for a less hierarchical approach. Peter Drucker advocated the empowerment of workers and Tom Peters highlighted the importance of companies creating learning cultures in which innovation is the norm and employees are focused on client satisfaction. In recent years these ideas have been refined into an approach known as *total quality management* (TQM), which is now being adapted to educational contexts. 'Total quality management is a philosophy with tools and processes for practical implementation aimed at achieving a culture of continuous improvement driven by all members of an organisation in order to satisfy and delight customers' (Marsh 1992).

The interest from many schools and LEAs in the Pacific Institute's 'Investment in Excellence' programme and efforts by others to become *Investors in People* indicates the current interest being shown in management systems which value and empower employees.

Total quality management is underpinned by the belief that an organization (in our case the school) should be focused on client satisfaction and that there is always scope for improvement in the service being provided. A second element of TQM is the idea that every organization has internal customers who also deserve a high quality service. Thus, in school, subject teams provide a service to pastoral teams

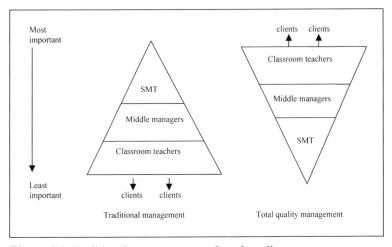

Figure 1.1 Traditional management and total quality management

and vice-versa. If a subject teacher fails to complete a report for a form tutor on time the service has fallen below an acceptable level and action is taken to address the problem. Finally, TQM involves the effective use of data to measure performance and establish targets for improvement.

In schools that have embraced an approach based on TQM there is a clear focus on client needs. The SMT and middle managers see their roles, in part, as serving colleagues at the chalk face as effectively as possible to enable them to provide a high quality learning experience for their pupils. Hierarchies are less in evidence. Teams are more fluid. Leadership roles are encouraged on the basis of knowledge and skill rather than position in the hierarchy. For example, a young teacher with good ICT skills could quite legitimately be encouraged to lead a working party investigating the use of ICT across the curriculum. They would be supported and assisted by more senior colleagues who would encourage a culture of collaboration. TQM schools systematically use data to provide evidence of how they are performing and are not frightened of asking probing questions about differences in performance between schools and teams within schools. At team level, similar questions are asked about differences in performance between teachers. This is not done to 'blame' particular teachers for poor performance but to establish reasons for under-performance and to address them.

Of course, this model can cause anxiety for teachers locked into the mentality of the rigid pyramid. Knowing 'where you stand' can provide a sense of security. Having to reflect on your performance can be threatening at first. However, there is now a wealth of evidence to suggest that pyramid schools are ill equipped to cope smoothly with change and that, by contrast, a 'collegiate' approach produces dynamic and adaptable institutions (see Chapter 3). This approach does not remove the need for middle managers but it does require of them a particular frame of mind. They must be capable of:

- monitoring levels of client satisfaction and responding to client needs;
- using data to analyse performance and plan for improvement;
- motivating and empowering colleagues in their teams to perform to their maximum potential;
- clear thinking and creative problem-solving.

It is likely that in the future these skills will become even more important, as the drive to improve school performance continues under a government committed to 'education, education, education'.

Good middle managers are not trapped in rigid strait-jackets but are flexible and adaptable, always on the lookout for ways to improve the education provided by their teams. They are able to move easily between roles – teacher, team leader, team member – as required. They gain satisfaction from empowering colleagues and seeing them succeed and constantly reflect on their own practice in the belief that better performance is always possible.

The context of middle management

Schools operate within particular localities and the local environment (geographical and social) is bound to influence the identity of the school. Likewise, schools are subject to national legislation and must operate within guidelines increasingly generated from central authorities. Most middle managers will have some responsibility for planning and monitoring the teaching of the national curriculum and organizing SATS, for example. However, it is a fact that schools in similar areas can create different cultures and levels of performance, as data from OFSTED inspections indicates. Likewise, within the same school, departments or teams may exhibit very different cultures and it is now clear from 'value-added' data that some departments perform much better than others in terms of examination results achieved by the pupils they teach. The message here is that middle managers can make a significant difference, even in schools lacking strong senior management direction and support.

Schools that embrace a management style that encourages excellence, initiative and flexibility are likely to be well equipped to face the future and a *collegiate* approach will be advocated throughout this book. However, most secondary schools, on paper at least, remain hierarchical face rebellion. Likewise, heads of department and curriculum leaders who promote differentiation at team meetings but don't apply differentiation in their own classroom will soon lose respect and credibility. This doesn't mean that middle managers must always be the best and most skilled teachers and good middle managers will acknowledge this. It does mean, however, that team leaders should set a good example in their practice and should not expect of colleagues what they cannot achieve themselves.

Two major areas of responsibility assigned to middle managers are subject and pastoral leadership. Job descriptions provide a somewhat clinical statement of what a given middle management job entails. Knowing what is required in practice is the key to interpreting a job description successfully. It is essential for middle managers to identify their roles in terms of

- tasks;
- responsibilities;
- relationships (internal and external).

In order to do this they must be clear about the management and communication structures in operation in their school and familiar with all school policies.

In practice, being an effective middle manager involves:

- *leading*, by being a role model for other staff;
- *serving* pupils, teachers and senior managers;
- *managing* the implementation of school and team aims and policies.

The art of getting the right balance can be elusive. Newly appointed middle managers often try so hard to serve that they neglect the managing dimension. In order to get things right *critical reflection* is essential and the ability to reflect also equips middle managers to solve effectively the many problems and dilemmas they will face.

Middle management is not easy. In some schools responsibility allowance holders can feel trapped between members of their team and the SMT as a result of conflicting expectations from these two groups of people. When teachers gain promotion internally to a middle management post, they take with them 'baggage' from their earlier roles and can sometimes find it quite stressful to settle into new relationships with colleagues. Sitting in any staff room and listening to conversations soon exposes team leaders who have not learnt the art of discretion. Professional integrity is very important for middle managers, as colleagues will only trust and respect them if they are certain that they can be approached in confidence.

Middle managers continually face role ambiguity and role conflict, with difficult choices to be made and, on occasions, difficult people to be confronted. How they approach such situations reflects on their integrity and often requires courage. Listening skills, sensitivity, reflection and persistence are all vital. The rewards of good middle management are visible in staff performance and pupil progress. It is also the case, in most schools, that good middle managers are respected and appreciated by junior and senior colleagues alike.

Middle managers are vital for the smooth running of a school. Responsibility posts can be exciting, rewarding and fulfilling. Hard-working and professional team leaders can make a real difference in a school. They can bring a unique ethos to a team, transform a lacklustre department and make a significant difference to pupil performance. Newly appointed and enthusiastic heads of year and heads of department often find that they serve as a catalyst, allowing a team to shape or rediscover its commitment and enthusiasm. Most teachers are reasonable people who respond positively to good leadership and want the best for their pupils. Effective middle managers are aware that they are a vital part of the drive to improve standards in schools, and their motivation, at least in part, comes from a desire to do the best they can for their pupils. 'Throughout their work (a middle manager) ensures that practices improve the quality of education provided, meet the needs and aspirations of all pupils and raise standards of achievement in school' (TTA 1998).

Peter Clarke, the head teacher who was instrumental in 'turning round' the troubled *Ridings School* in Halifax, accepts this view and acknowledges the vital role middle managers play in effective schools. 'Successful management of schools requires effective middle managers who take responsibility for managing their teams and achieving objectives ... strong middle managers become the "engine room" of the school, taking initiatives and making decisions' (Clarke 1998).

Case studies

Below are two imaginary situations. Read each one and reflect on it from a management perspective. Think about the failures of middle (and senior) managers in these cases. How would you have dealt with each case? When you are clear about what you think read the reflections on the case studies.

Case 1

John Smith is a 30-year-old History teacher with eight years' teaching experience, all in his present school. He is a knowledgeable teacher who gained a good first degree but ever since his none-too-successful first year in the school, his head of department and year head have carefully selected only the most amenable groups for him to teach. He seems unaware of the poor reputation for discipline he has acquired. When he is 'on duty' or 'covering' for absent colleagues, John faces serious problems. His head of department has employed a strategy of 'working round' John and playing to his strength, which is academic teaching.

John is a caring tutor, though he is disorganized in matters of administration and his pupils sometimes 'take him for a ride'. Generally, though, his relationships with them are good. He takes an active part in school social activities and is usually very cooperative. He has done little sustained INSET since he joined the school and has never volunteered to lead any new initiatives.

John's head of department has indicated his intention to apply for early retirement. John has approached the head teacher with a request to be considered for the job. He feels he is the natural successor if an internal appointment is to be made, and he cites his excellent subject knowledge and first degree as evidence of his suitability for the job.

Where have school managers gone wrong with John?
What would you have done?

Reflection

It is possible to identify failures on the part of both middle and senior managers in this situation, which tells us something about the culture of the school. The following points should have been noted:

- Poor use of the first year of teaching to identify weaknesses and begin a programme of training suggests inadequate induction, monitoring and mentoring.
- Managers preferring to 'work round' John's weaknesses rather than helping him to address them suggests lack of courage and determination on the part of middle managers and more senior colleagues.
- John's failure to realize his own weaknesses and to be aware that running a department takes more than subject knowledge suggests that both appraisal and professional development have been ineffective in this school.

John might be a very different teacher at 30 if:

- his head of department had worked closely with him to improve approaches to discipline and develop his teaching skills with less academic children;
- his year leader had insisted on and supported him in efficient administration;

- senior staff had not ignored problems facing John when on duty and on cover;
- the school had in place regular staff reviews so that John's career plans were known and training towards subject headship had been provided;
- INSET in the school was linked to identified needs of teachers.

Clearly, there was failure of management at many levels. John did not reflect critically on his performance but it would be wrong to blame him entirely for his failings. He is obviously a willing and cooperative teacher with some identifiable strengths. Through their failure to address his weaknesses, John has been let down by management, who have created problems for themselves by 'working round' him. If he is now appointed as head of History, he is unlikely to do the job effectively. If he is not appointed, he may well become disgruntled and withdraw his goodwill. Taking what seemed like the easy way out may prove costly for this school in the long run.

Case 2

A GCSE pupil approaches the head of Business Studies, Mrs Brown, with a complaint. Miss Smith (his Business Studies teacher) has lost his GCSE assignment, he claims. He gave it to her in her form room but she says he has not handed it in. He is annoyed and says that it is not the first time she has lost work belonging to pupils in the class. Also, he says, Miss Smith doesn't explain things clearly when he asks for help and never bothers to mark their books. He produces his exercise book to substantiate his claim.

The head of department goes to Miss Smith, who teaches part-time and is rarely in school. She mentions the missing assignment but not the unmarked book and Miss Smith responds aggressively. She says the boy never handed the work in and accuses him of being arrogant, always expecting special attention in class. She also says the class concerned is disruptive and uncooperative. She says she is simply not prepared to work herself into an early grave for such children who 'know their rights but not their responsibilities'. She blames the head of department for giving her such a bad group and says she is suffering stress because of it.

Mrs Brown talks to the boy's year head. Apparently, he is a bright and confident youngster who will do well in his GCSEs. It is true that the group he is in needs careful handling because it contains several difficult pupils, but they are certainly not the worst group in the year as far as behaviour goes.

Mrs Brown tells the boy he must do his assignment again. She says she believes Miss Smith's version of events. She discusses with Miss Smith the possibility of moving some disruptive pupils out of her GCSE class into her own group.

Where has the head of department gone wrong?
What would you have done?

Reflection

It is possible to identify many mistakes made by the head of Business Studies. The fact that a pupil was able to come to her with accusations of lost work, books not marked and problems with teaching suggests she does not know what is going on in her department. The best of teachers can, of course, lose work occasionally, but this situation is more serious as Miss Smith is clearly very stressed and appears to be failing the pupils in several respects.

We might well ask:

- Does the head of Business Studies liaise with the year head when putting pupils into GCSE groups to avoid creating problem classes?
- Is there a system in place for monitoring the performance of pupils in GCSE Business Studies so that underachievement is quickly identified?
- Does the head of Business Studies have a way of monitoring such things as the marking of books?
- Why has Miss Smith not felt able to approach Mrs Brown about the difficulties she has encountered?
- Has Mrs Brown tried to set up a regular meeting time with Miss Smith to ensure she feels valued as part of the team, even though she is part-time?
- Does Mrs Brown observe members of her team in the classroom so that she is aware of their strengths and weaknesses?

Of course, the culture of the school will, to an extent, determine the way the heads of department operate. In this example, as in the last, a 'hands-off' or 'easy-life' approach has been adopted. Bad practice has gone unnoticed or unquestioned. There has been a failure of management.

There are other points to pick up from this case study. It is worth considering them from the point of view of the clients:

- The pupil has been treated badly. He will feel resentful towards the school. He may fail to repeat the assignment and this will effect his GCSE result. He may involve his parents. This may create the need to involve a senior member of staff. If the parents feel badly treated they will speak ill of the school to their friends and neighbours. This may influence whether or not they send their children to the school.

Worse still, the boy may decide to attend a different school to study A levels.

- Miss Smith has not been served well. Removing a few difficult children from her class is a 'quick-fix' but it does not address her failure to mark books and the problems she is experiencing in the classroom. She is stressed and feels angry. Her head of department has not explored these issues. If Miss Smith is not supported she could end up taking time off work due to ill health and more serious problems could then follow.

In this case, ineffective middle management could result in the school losing pupils and the revenue they bring with them. It should have been possible to treat the pupil more positively and support him in repeating his assignment. Miss Smith needed support and her weaknesses should not have gone unnoticed for so long. The biggest failure in management was that so many things were happening that the head of department was unaware of.

Summary

Over the past twenty years management theory and practice has been adapted and applied to the education system, with the aim of improving the achievement of young people and making schools more accountable. There is clear evidence that better management is helping to improve standards in schools and for this reason there is currently a drive towards enhancing the management skills of middle management in secondary schools.

Schools taking a collegiate approach to management operate flexibly, empowering teachers to be creative (but also accountable) and use their skills and talents to improve the education of the young people they serve. Such schools have a clear client focus and encourage collective responsibility. When things go wrong blame is shared and people work together to find solutions. Such schools are proving to be better at coping with change than more rigid, hierarchical organizations.

Middle managers in any secondary school are concerned with creating a clear sense of purpose for their department or year group; managing teams of people, individuals and other resources effectively to achieve agreed targets; and ensuring that routine administration is efficient and effective. In schools where total quality management or a similar philosophy is being encouraged middle managers are engaged in developing a clear client focus and in ensuring that internal customers, as well as pupils, parents and other client groups, are provided with a good quality of service.

Middle managers play many roles and need to be able to adapt comfortably to each role. As teachers, team leaders and team members they need to behave appropriately and display a level of commitment and integrity deserving of respect. Middle managers lead by example; they are active in helping to shape the school's mission while at the same time being sensitive to the pressures faced by classroom teachers. Good middle managers develop clear reflective thinking as a means of solving problems they encounter and to help them to be more proactive in the shaping of events.

All middle managers face challenges, demands, dilemmas and obstacles. At times they can feel frustrated and even demoralized but it is also the case that middle management can be exciting, challenging, rewarding and fulfilling. Middle managers who help a team or department create a clear identity and group loyalty, develop a sense of purpose and begin to make a real difference in the quality of education provided feel rightly proud.

The satisfaction middle managers get out of their roles can usually be equated to the effort they put in.

CHAPTER TWO

Different Management Styles

Introduction

While it is obvious that all human beings are unique individuals it is also true that certain traits common to large numbers of people make it possible to group similar individuals together and predict their behaviour. Social scientists have studied common traits and the predictability of behaviour in order to classify people according to personality, social class, cultural group and so on. It is now generally felt that the behaviour we observe in individuals is a product of genetic make-up, social learning and the contexts in which individuals operate. This is as true for managers as it is for any other social group.

Despite knowing this, when talking to middle managers about how they approach their work I am still amazed by how easy it is to fit them into particular categories, according to their predominant management style. Likewise, when working with teachers aspiring to middle management posts, the introduction of typologies of management style into a teaching session usually results in an immediate conversion to the usefulness of management theory. This is simply because teachers can instantly recognize the managers they work with in the models, and this seems to assist them in understanding the reasons for the success or lack of success of the managers they know.

It is certainly very useful to analyse the various styles of management uncovered by management theorists and reflect on their utility in the secondary school context. Before doing this, however, it is important to consider the following points:

- Management style is not fixed. While certain personalities are more likely to approach the management of others in a particular way, everyone can learn new ways of managing people. The important thing is to be open-minded and self-critical. If you are pre-disposed to a particular style of management, but there is clear evidence that other styles seem to be more effective, then the good manager will learn to use the features of the style that is known to work.

- Different situations require different management styles. Good managers are able to adjust their approach to suit the task, the context and the individuals with whom they are working. Even when there is evidence that a particular style of management is *usually* effective there may well be circumstances in which other styles are needed to produce the required results. Being able to assess which situation requires which style is critical.
- Middle managers work in teams. By knowing the personalities of your team you will be able to use the skills of others to complement your style of management. Again, this requires honesty and critical reflection. Don't be afraid to use the strengths of others; knowing more about management styles will help you to assess yourself and see how others in your team can be used to complement your particular strengths. Skilled managers make this look easy, but it is something young managers often struggle with, believing, wrongly, that they should be capable of being all things to all people. A degree of humility, coupled to the ability to make others feel valued for their particular strengths, is what makes many team leaders in secondary school successful.

Models of management

Research on management styles has identified clear traits and management theorists have assembled these traits into typologies of management style and management models. A number of these models are identified in this chapter. Some of the models, naturally, have similarities, and a synthesis of the models can help in reaching a clear understanding of the key characteristics of managers you know and of yourself as a manager.

The authoritarian/laissez-faire axis

One simple model of management places all managers somewhere on a continuum from *authoritarian* to *laissez-faire*, with most managers showing traits that place them in one of the following groups:

AUTHORITARIAN   DEMOCRATIC   LAISSEZ-FAIRE

The groups are based on an analysis of how managers behave towards the people who work in their teams. At one end of the scale are authoritarian managers (dictators who need to control all aspects of a team's work) and at the other end of the scale are laissez-faire managers (who seem happy to allow colleagues to do just as they please). In the middle are democratic managers who share a clear sense of purpose with team members and involve colleagues in deciding the most appropriate ways of achieving agreed goals.

Most managers, if honest, will admit their approach resembles one of these positions. Certainly, people working in their teams rarely have any difficulty in identifying their style of management as the characteristics displayed are easy to identify (see Table 2.1).

Authoritarian	Democratic	Laissez-faire
• Tells people what to do • Keeps information from team members • Stifles debate • Tightly controls meetings • Gives the impressions that decisions are made before they are discussed • Employs rigid procedures • Seems to have 'tunnel vision' • Fails to develop colleagues by refusing to delegate	• Directs or supports people as necessary • Shares information of relevance to the team • Plans well-structured meetings which allow for debate but reach decisions • Agrees clear procedures with the team • Has a clear philosophy but listens to other views • Develops colleagues by negotiating the delegation of some tasks	• Doesn't like directing people • Shares information unnecessarily • Allows so much debate that clear decisions are rarely made • Allows meetings to drag on • Lacks procedures • Gives the impression of having no clear philosophy for the team • Fails to develop colleagues by not planning delegation

Table 2.1 Authoritarian, democratic and laissez-faire managers

The MacGregor X–Y axis

While the laissez-faire approach amounts to a failure to manage, the authoritarian and democratic typologies seem to reflect conflicting underlying assumptions about human nature and how people should be treated in order to get the most out of them in a work situation. The American management consultant, Douglas MacGregor, first identified two extreme and opposing sets of beliefs held by managers in his book *The Human Side of Management* (McGraw Hill, 1960). MacGregor's categories are given in Table 2.2.

MacGregor X thinking	*MacGregor Y thinking*
• People are naturally lazy	• People are naturally motivated
• People are not interested in improving their performance	• People want to do well and improve their performance
• People need supervision	• People want to take responsibility
• People can't be trusted with making decisions	• People thrive on being involved in decision making

Table 2.2   MacGregor X and MacGregor Y thinking

Newtonian and Whiteheadian managers

There are echoes of the MacGregor axis in the more recent materials developed by the Pacific Institute for their 'Investment in Excellence' programme, now being widely applied in education and other public-service organizations. According to Louis Tice (Pacific Institute 1997) people can be classed as either Newtonian or Whiteheadian, depending on how they see the world. These views of the world (set out in table 2.3) can have a profound influence on the way they manage others.

Isaac Newton, in the seventeenth century, was deeply interested in religion. Through his scientific work he wanted to show the order which existed in God's universe. He believed that the world was entirely predictable except for human beings, who represented a threat to God's creation. Therefore, according to Newtonian logic, human beings must be controlled. In organizational terms this means people must know their place, must have rigid procedures to follow and must not be given the autonomy to take risks. Managers are there to keep people on-task and prevent them working against their employers and disrupting the smooth running of the organization.

Alfred North Whitehead (1861–1947) was a mathematician physicist and a philosopher whose world-view was very different. In contrast to Newton, he believed that God was working to make a better world. Far from being a threat to God's ordered world human beings were, in fact, capable of inventing better ways of doing things; they were helping to move the world towards perfection. Applied to organizations a Whiteheadian approach results in people having more autonomy and accountability being spread throughout the organization. The job of management is to empower people to achieve the goals of the organization creatively. Far from being seen as a threat the workers are seen as the key resource of an organization.

Newtonian managers	Whiteheadian managers
• Assume a basically stable environment	• Assume constant change
• Assume people are basically lazy and incompetent	• Believe people can be creative and inventive
• Think control must come from above	• Think control should be shared
• Think only managers are accountable	• Think accountability should be shared
• Get self-esteem from power and position	• Get self-esteem from supporting and nurturing others
• Think people work best when given set tasks	• Think flexible people are more useful

Table 2.3 Newtonian and Whiteheadian managers

During the last twenty years more and more organizations, including public-service industries, have embraced the Whiteheadian perspective. Through initiatives such as *Investors in People* the importance of developing individual potential so that people can contribute to the organization has been acknowledged. Research into school effectiveness has demonstrated the benefits of involving all staff in planning and decision-making and encouraging both greater autonomy and accountability. Put simply, schools taking a Whiteheadian approach to management seem to be more dynamic and successful. Middle managers, therefore, would be advised to take such an approach with their teams, though this is clearly more difficult for team leaders working in a Newtonian school. Whiteheadian middle managers working in Newtonian schools would need gradually to change the culture of their teams as Newtonian team members are likely to be over-dependent on their managers. These themes will be expanded in Chapter 3 when effective cultures are explored.

Task-orientated managers and people-orientated managers

Another way of classifying managers is to place them on a continuum somewhere between the extremes of *people-orientated* and *task-orientated*.

PEOPLE–ORIENTATED _____ TASK–ORIENTATED

Managers who are strongly task-orientated tend to be good at planning and administration. They are often efficient and can be relied on to 'get

21

the job done'. However, the downside of being strongly task-orientated is a tendency to lack tolerance for those who are unable to work as efficiently as the team leader and a frustration with those who challenge plans being put into action. Task-orientated managers are often seen as aloof and can sometimes fail to consult colleagues, being over-zealous about 'getting on with it'.

In contrast, people-orientated managers tend to be much less bothered about planning and administrative efficiency and much more concerned with keeping up the morale of people in their team. They are usually prepared to devote a great deal of time to listening and feel that consulting colleagues is an essential aspect of management. Strongly people-orientated managers can sometimes spend so much time on 'keeping people happy' that they neglect to move their team forward towards achieving agreed goals.

Of course, a successful manager is someone who can combine a concern for people with administrative efficiency and the ability to get things done. In reality, most middle managers fall somewhere between the two extremes mentioned, and it is certainly possible for managers with a tendency to one extreme or the other to compensate for this by conscious effort based on critical reflection and the learning of new skills.

There are, in fact, similarities between the 'people-task' model of management and the 'authoritarian-laissez-faire' model. Managers who fail to consult and are obsessed with administrative systems are sure to be seen as authoritarian by colleagues. Likewise, managers who are so concerned about the different views and feelings of colleagues that they are never able to lead a team to a consensus or a clear decision end up, even if unintentionally, being laissez-faire managers.

Figure 2.1 illustrates the links between some of the management characteristics mentioned earlier in the chapter and the people-task classification.

Position A managers are strong on people but weak on task. They are fair and considerate to people, trusting them to be professional and get on with their jobs. Such managers may, however, fail to give a clear sense of direction and may also fail to develop the skills and potential of those in their team. With a highly motivated and highly skilled team, in a fairly stable organization, it is possible for *people managers* of this type to be successful.

Position B managers are very efficient and well-organized, with a clear sense of what needs doing to move their team or department forward. However, it is likely that such managers do not adequately involve colleagues in deciding on goals or ways of achieving goals. B managers may be irritated by people in the team who do not share or understand the goals and are unlikely to be sympathetic to people slowing down the

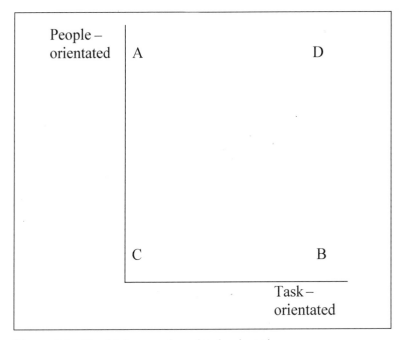

Figure 2.1 Combining people and task orientation

process of change. In rigid, hierarchical organizations there are plenty of these *authoritarian managers*. Arguably, such people can be useful as middle managers in schools, when particular tasks need accomplishing quickly and efficiently. However, schools are people-orientated organizations that depend on teams working together and individuals being nurtured to perform to the best of their ability. For this reason B managers are of only limited value.

Position C managers are weak on both task and people skills and as such fail to manage at all. C managers are *laissez-faire managers* of the worst kind, being unable to get tasks done but also leaving colleagues to their own devices with no concern or support being offered. In most schools, thankfully, laissez-faire managers are becoming extinct, as the pressure of constant change, greater accountability and regular inspection makes it impossible for such individuals to survive.

Position D managers are able to combine the ability to accomplish tasks with a genuine concern for colleagues. Such managers have clear goals and clear ideas about how to move towards those goals. In addition, D managers are capable of engaging other team members in deciding on how goals can be achieved and are supportive of colleagues who encounter difficulties with change. D managers are good listeners, make effective use of the skills of people in their team and are flexible. Above all else D managers are able to keep the morale of the team high and, by so doing, enable the team to reach agreed goals. Such expert managers are best described as *omega managers*. They have clear potential for school leadership.

Management styles and fitness for purpose?

The problem with looking at models of management style is that they distort reality. While most managers display traits which make it easy to place them in a particular category, it is likely that most authoritarian managers have some people skills and most people-orientated managers have some planning ability and an awareness of tasks to be done. The important thing is that managers are realistic and honest about their strengths and weaknesses as a starting point for improving management performance.

I well recall a management training session with a group of middle and senior managers from the same school which illustrates this point. When the course members were working in small groups on management styles it soon became clear to me that just about all the middle managers had identified a member of their senior management team as being a textbook example of an authoritarian manager. This senior manager was present at the training session and was telling members of the group he was working with how well he thought he fitted the democratic model of management.

This massive gap between the assessment made by his colleagues and the self-assessment of this particular manager rang alarm bells for me, because of the potential for friction in the school concerned which could arise out of these two contrasting versions of his behaviour. It is important that managers are genuinely self-critical and make themselves aware of how they are seen by others. Armed with this knowledge it is possible to begin working on areas of weakness in order to become a better and more rounded manager. Adair (1997) sums up the importance of understanding how others perceive you rather amusingly as follows:

> If one person says that you are a horse,
> Smile at them.
> If two people say that you are a horse,
> Give it some thought.
> If three people say that you are a horse,
> Go out and buy a saddle.

It is also vital to realize that using a style of management *fit for purpose* is also very important. When the school fire bell goes it is essential that even managers who are highly people-orientated snap into an authoritarian mode, for everybody's sake. Having a meeting about how people feel about evacuating the building would clearly be ludicrous. More serious examples are easy to find. A newly appointed middle manager, facing an OFSTED inspection and needing to get various things in place, may need to use a task-orientated style, even though they may be committed to a more democratic approach in the long run.

Different styles of management may also be needed for different people. While a democratic, people-friendly approach may be the most effective style of management for colleagues who are committed and professional, a more authoritarian style may have to be used with colleagues who are uncooperative and deliberately obstructive, if all else fails. Depending on the level of skill of people in a team, managers may find themselves *directing, coaching, supporting* or *delegating* in order to get the best out of each individual. This theme will be explored in Chapter 4.

Just as good middle managers make effective use of the strengths of individuals in their team so good senior managers will be aware of, and use appropriately, the strengths of their middle managers. I can think of one school where the job of writing the school's timetable was delegated to a very task-orientated middle manager. However, to ensure that people's views were not ignored in the process of timetable construction, a deputy with very strong people skills held regular meetings between the timetable writer and other team leaders, to ensure that consultation was thorough and decisions made were fair. In another institution the review of the school's approach to Equal Opportunities was delegated to a middle manager with strong people skills. She was able to create the right sort of ethos in meetings, which allowed for very different views to be expressed openly and debated in a non-threatening way. These two examples show the importance of using people's strengths and ensuring *fitness for purpose,* with the aim of creating an organization that effectively meets the needs of its students. 'Effective management is about working with and through others in order to maximise impact where it most benefits all pupils. It is about enabling things to happen, empowering colleagues and helping to establish the necessary conditions' (West 1997) .

Case studies

Below are the imaginary reflections of two newly qualified teachers following a half term in their new jobs. They are set out in the form of a conversation between the two. What do their views tell us about the management style of their heads of department?

'Well, my first half term at Leafy Glades Comprehensive certainly has been a baptism by fire. I feel ready for a good rest. Don't misunderstand me, the pupils are generally fine. There are a few lively characters, of course, but I met youngsters worse than them on TP. It's the department that leaves a lot to be desired!'

'What do you mean? Don't you get on with your head of department?'

'It isn't as though my head of department isn't supportive. In fact, he's very friendly indeed. It's just that he doesn't seem to have got his act together and, as such, the department seems really disorganized. I do get on with my head of department; he's not at all aloof, but he doesn't really behave like my head of department on TP.'

'What do you mean?'

'Well, on teaching practice my head of department was my mentor and gave really good, practical advice. I thought that this would continue during my first year of teaching but Chris, my new head of department, just leaves me to get on with it. He asks me how I'm doing but we never really talk in detail about my teaching. I've no idea how well I'm doing really. Chris praises me but he seems to praise everyone all the time, so I don't read too much in to that. Another thing, I've asked for a departmental handbook on several occasions, only to be told that it is being rewritten, and the so-called schemes of work I was provided with are little more than lists of topics. Frankly, I feel the schemes I wrote on my last TP are better, but I can hardly tell Chris that.'

'What about the other teachers in the team, are they just as bad?'

'It's difficult to say as I hardly see them. You see, there's no real departmental base and the History teachers only seem to get together once a fortnight when departmental meetings are scheduled.'

'At least you have regular meetings, then?'

'Yes, but they don't accomplish much. I've not yet seen an agenda, people seem to wander in at whatever time they like so we never start the meetings on time. In fact, the head of department is usually late himself. He's usually been talking to some pupil about their work. That's part of the problem, I think, he tries to be helpful to everyone, but his organization is weak. He doesn't seem to have any sense of priorities. For example, when a meeting does eventually get underway people will chip in with all kinds of issues and anecdotes and the really important things seem to get forgotten. I find it very frustrating and I get anxious about the lack of clear decisions. The others seem to cope with it, though. They've been at the school a long time and just seem to do their own thing. I think I'd call it "muddling through". I do feel dreadful speaking about Chris like this, as he really is a very caring person. His heart is in the right place. He even sent me a card at the end of my first half term, thanking me for my hard work.'

'That is nice. I don't think Julie, my head of department, would do that. She sounds like the complete opposite of your Chris.'

'In what sense?'

'Well, the department really is very well organized. You'll remember how impressed I was with that when I went for interview at Green Meadows: detailed schemes of work, the same textbooks for everyone to use, immaculate wall displays and so on. But Julie is not what I would call a warm person. I don't think I could turn to her if I had a personal problem and she is rather thin with her praise.'

'That's so different to Leafy Glades, I wish we had some clear direction on which books to use.'

'Yes, but it can go too far. I feel as though I have no freedom to experiment. After all, part of being a teacher is using your judgement about what a class needs. I used to enjoy preparing teaching materials on TP but Julie doesn't encourage that. In fact, she observed a lesson where I'd prepared a brilliant worksheet but she said I should have stuck to the textbook. She started going on about the cost of printing worksheets, which left me feeling rather deflated.'

'Is Julie obsessed with not over-spending, then?'

'I'm not sure. I think it might have more to do with not wanting her team to deviate from agreed schemes of work. This comes across in meetings. They are so well organized but rigid. We always have an agenda and everyone turns up on time but there isn't any real discussion. People listen to Julie giving instructions; there's no real debate. I think people find it difficult to criticize Julie because she seems to work so hard. She prepares such detailed documents and schemes I just can't believe she has time for any life beyond school.'

'My head of department certainly has a social life. He's quite happy to share that with colleagues.'

'Julie is a perfectionist. She's devoted to her job and she expects everyone else to be the same. I've felt very pressurized this term because of it. She seems to be scrutinizing my work more closely than my mentor on TP did, which hasn't exactly boosted my confidence. In fact, on one occasion I hadn't remembered to return a set of textbooks to the store room and she got really quite shirty about it.'

'I've just had a funny thought.'

'What's that?'

'Maybe we'll be heads of department one day and NQTs will be pulling us to pieces like this.'

'Yes, but hopefully we'll learn from the likes of Chris and Julie and make a better job of things.'

Reflection

While Chris and Julie are imaginary characters, managers similar to both of them exist in many schools. Chris displays many of the characteristics associated with a laissez-faire manager and Julie seems strongly task-

Chris

Strengths	Weaknesses
• Caring	• Lacks organizational skills
• Kind	• Lacks time-management skills
• Thoughtful	• Fails to prioritize
• Presents a human face to colleagues	• Fails to usefully involve colleagues
	• Fails to provide *useful* support
	• Fails to give a sense of direction
	• Fails to develop team members

Table 2.4   Chris: strengths and weaknesses

Julie

Strengths	Weaknesses
• Hard-working and efficient	• Lacks flexibility
• Good at administration	• Lacks empathy
• Good organizational skills	• Fails to build confidence in team members
• Gives clear instructions	• Fails to provide *useful* support
• Has a clear sense of direction	• Fails to develop team members
	• Fails to usefully involve colleagues

Table 2.5   Julie: strengths and weaknesses

orientated. Both have strengths as well as weaknesses. It is worth reflecting on these strengths and weaknesses (see tables 2.4 and 2.5).

There may well be other points you have noted which could be added to these lists. The interesting thing is that both managers are failing to develop their teams, provide effective support and usefully involve colleagues, despite their very different styles. Both managers could improve. Chris needs management training in organization and communication as a priority, and Julie needs to be introduced to people management and team-building. Before this could happen, of course, both would need to be genuinely self-critical and want to improve their performance. We should also note that the senior managers at Leafy Glades and Green Meadows seem to have been less than effective if two middle managers with such easily identifiable weaknesses exist. Appraisal and staff development in these schools seems not to have been taken seriously.

Summary

A number of different management styles have been identified and these styles are easily recognizable in school contexts. Some managers have a tendency towards being *authoritarian* and *task-orientated* while others seem to be more *people-centred*. The most successful managers are those who can combine effective planning for the achievement of clear goals, with a style of managing people that is supportive and motivating. This is especially important for middle managers in schools, who regularly find themselves having to lead their teams towards goals set externally by senior managers or central authorities.

Generally, a style of management that involves others in decision-making and empowers individuals to use their talents to achieve goals is most effective. However, different styles of management are appropriate for different tasks and in different contexts. Good managers will be flexible about the styles they use and will learn to slip between styles depending on the task they are undertaking and the people they are dealing with. Thus, the ability to reflect and analyse is very important for managers who want to ensure that the approach they use is *fit for purpose*.

Managers operate in the way they do because of a combination of personality, training, institutional culture and immediate context. All managers are capable of learning new skills and it is possible for determined managers to enhance their performance. To do this, though, they must be open, honest and self-critical. They must involve others in appraising their performance so that they begin to see themselves as others see them. Only then will they be able to begin to develop those aspects of their management which need development.

Good managers see it as a duty to develop the skills of people in the teams they lead. By using the abilities of others, effective managers can often compensate for weaknesses they acknowledge in themselves. Middle managers should not feel threatened by others in their teams who have skills and attributes they lack, but should see these people as a rich human resource to be used to the benefit of the school and the children in the school. It is very often managers who are unsure of their abilities who find humility difficult. Those who are confident about their strengths and abilities will have less difficulty in helping others shine and develop.

CHAPTER THREE

A Look at Effective School Cultures

Introduction

In the course of my work I get the opportunity to visit many schools. What I find interesting is just how different schools with comparable intakes of pupils can be. It would be easy to assume that schools in similar areas would be very much the same, given that they all have to deliver the national curriculum and that they serve similar parents and cater for similar types of students. This is simply not the case: on walking into some schools the positive ethos is palpable, whereas in others a very different atmosphere exists. This is not simply a matter of the appearance of the buildings or the layout of the reception area, it is about the culture that the organization has developed and lives by.

When you enter a school and feel a positive ethos and sense a real culture of cooperation and achievement you can be sure that this doesn't exist by accident. It is likely to be the result of a vision shared by all staff, good selection and training procedures and effective policies which give staff and students a clear sense of direction, together with considerable autonomy and responsibility. It is likely that in these schools staff have high expectations of students and each other and that there is a strong belief in involving students in decisions about their learning. These schools have usually embraced some aspects of a total quality management approach (see Chapter 1), especially the importance of believing that both internal and external clients are deserving of a high-quality service. In addition, staff collaboration is likely to be well developed. It is possible to be fairly confident about these claims, as there is now a wealth of research evidence to support the notion that some school cultures are more effective than others.

Some thoughts on culture

As school culture or ethos seems to be so important it is worth being clear about its meaning. *Culture* in its broadest sense can be defined as the 'way of life' of an entire society. This includes the codes of manners, dress, language, rituals, norms and beliefs held by people in the society in question. Within societies there are also *sub-cultures*: a system of beliefs, values and norms shared by an appreciable minority of people within a particular culture.

Just as societies can be analysed and explained in terms of cultures and sub-cultures so can organizations, where culture can be seen as 'an amalgam of the values, norms and beliefs that characterise the way in which a group of people behave within a specific organisational setting' (Ainscow 1994) Middle managers in all walks of life, including education, operate in the context of wider organizational cultures, which influence and restrain their actions; encouraging some forms of behaviour and making others more difficult. Just as in wider society, organizations can contain sub-cultural groups, operating in ways that are at odds with the dominant culture. It is important for team leaders in secondary schools to be aware of this basic organizational sociology, as many of the challenges they face and frustrations they feel will be able to be explained through a consideration of organizational cultures and sub-cultures.

Considerable research has been undertaken and much has now been written about school cultures but it is important to bear two things in mind as the evidence is considered:

- First, schools exist to prepare students for adult life. Most teachers would accept that they have a duty to do the best they can for each child both in terms of exam results and in helping them to develop an outlook that will enable them to become responsible and active citizens in a democratic country. The culture of a school has a direct bearing on both of these aims and that is why getting the culture right is so important. 'The challenge is to move schools to develop responsive cultures for the moral purpose of more effectively working with students and parents to enhance the level of student learning' (Davies and West-Burnham 1997).
- Secondly, there is now much evidence from OFSTED reports and other sources to show that even in schools where the dominant culture leaves much to be desired, sub-cultures and even individual teachers can thrive, working in ways that are more effective and which result in higher achievement levels for their students. Team leaders who find themselves in badly managed schools can take heart from this. While it is difficult to swim against the tide real progress

is possible and effective team leaders can become real *change agents* in a school. With regular inspections now a feature of the education system, all schools are rising to the challenge of developing cultures which match those of the most successful schools, and outdated and ineffective school cultures, like the dinosaurs, will simply not survive this process of evolution.

Organizational cultures

Handy and Aitken (1986) and Fullan and Hargreaves (1992) have identified a number of cultures relating to schools as organizations. Aspects of these cultures can still be found in many schools and they provide a useful starting point for middle managers wanting to reflect on the functioning of the organization in which they work. When considering these cultures do bear in mind that, as with leadership styles, the pure form may not exist, as schools will reflect these cultures in varying degrees. However, organizations are likely to display distinct traits from one or more of these cultures and there is likely to be a dominant culture or ethos, best summed up as 'the way we do things around here'.

The role culture

Here the organization is traditional and hierarchical. There are clear job descriptions and role boundaries, formalized communication and procedures and an emphasis on individuals keeping to their area of expertise. Schools that fit this model are usually well managed but not necessarily led by people with vision. They are efficient and well suited to a stable world, but schools of this type are not well equipped for coping with the rapid changes that are now a permanent feature of education.

The club culture

Here the organization has a head teacher who cultivates the support of like-minded colleagues. Circles of intimates develop and can have greater influence than formal post holders who fall outside the 'club'. The head in such schools often uses power in an arbitrary way, rather than following agreed procedures; decisions are often made informally through discussions with the 'in-crowd' and few things are written down. Such organizations can be exciting places to work for people who have the head's patronage but other colleagues can feel marginalized and unimportant. The nepotism that exists in these schools is certainly unfair and works against principles of equal opportunities and the reliance placed on the head teacher is very unhealthy. While the club culture is more common in primary schools many secondary teachers would argue that aspects of the club culture are evident in their schools also.

The task culture

Warmth, friendliness and cooperation with little evidence of hierarchy are features of the task culture. People work as teams and groups can be changed or disbanded as the task changes. Such cultures aid problem-solving and enable all individuals to contribute to moving the organization forward. There is open questioning of past procedures and a commitment to improving the services provided. Young, energetic and self-confident people thrive in such communities. Some schools display many aspects of the task culture and particular teams and departments in secondary schools can certainly be classified in this group. The task culture is liked neither by people who cling to job titles for security nor by people who feel threatened by 'young blood'.

The person culture

In organizations where a person culture exists professional autonomy is seen as important. The organization allows individuals to display their talents and managers interfere as little as possible, leaving the 'experts' to get on with the job. Professionals are persuaded, influenced, cajoled and bargained with but not commanded or instructed. Teachers working in schools thirty years ago had autonomy, and procedures and monitoring which are now commonplace would have been anathemas. While the person culture in its pure form is now very rare there are still echoes of it which, in part, explains why some managers are still very reluctant to challenge the behaviour of some colleagues, even when their performance is of an unacceptable level.

The individualistic culture

Here people work in isolation. There is little collaboration and sharing of ideas and people rarely receive feedback on performance. People avoid innovation and risk-taking and new ideas are not embraced. Individuals do not seek or welcome help and there is little incentive to improve performance, even though individuals may have high expectations of themselves. When meetings do take place few people contribute and even interaction at a social level is rare. There is a real danger that in very large schools, where departments do not have base areas and staff meetings are unproductive, individualized cultures can develop.

The balkanized culture

In balkanized schools teachers develop loyalty to separate groups and there is competition between groups. Departments behave like nation states and distinct sub-cultures exist which make working with a common ethos difficult. There is a lack of communication between groups and a tendency to assume negative stereotypes about members of other groups. Conflict over time, rooms, resources and exam option systems are common. In balkanized schools making a success of whole-school initiatives is very difficult.

The collaborative culture

In schools where a collaborative culture exists there is a clear and shared vision about the values and purposes of the school and this vision is regularly reviewed and examined. Teachers' voices are strong, disagreements are visible and teachers are both empowered and accountable. Team teaching and joint planning are common, teachers are willing to be learners and there is a commitment to ongoing professional development. Teams work effectively and there is a high level of trust and openness. Hierarchies are not so obvious and banter, jokes and celebrations reflect mutual understanding and respect.

As you consider these cultures it is worth thinking about the following questions:

- Which culture do you associate with the organization you work in?
- Can more than one culture be present in the same organization?
- In which culture would change occur most easily?
- What effect would each of these cultures have on students?
- Which school culture would generate the most positive school ethos?
- How can middle managers help to change the school culture?

Clearly, schools which are successful in today's educational world are those which can respond to change effectively. The task culture and the club culture would seem most appropriate for this. However, as we have seen, the club culture is unlikely to get the best out of *all* colleagues. Although the era of the person culture as described above has now passed, many successful heads try to provide autonomy for their staff, set in the context of clear goals and a strategic vision, as a way of creating a dynamic culture. The collaborative culture best fits the evidence emerging about successful schools and it is the approach currently being promoted in much literature on school effectiveness and through management training.

At the heart of the collaborative culture is the idea that schools can only develop and improve through the creative involvement of all those who work in them. The unfortunate divide which has emerged in some schools between 'managers' and 'teachers' needs to be broken down so that all can contribute their skills to achieving an agreed vision. This *empowerment* helps to generate commitment and means that all teachers, regardless of their job title, can contribute their skills and enthusiasm to moving a school forward.

> An important aspect of the character of effective schools is that management is not the unique task of those at the apex of a hierarchy but a shared responsibility of all who are involved in the school. A culture which proclaims that heads (and deputies) manage but teachers teach is not conducive to effective development. (Hargreaves and Hopkins 1991)

Linking this to management styles considered in Chapter 2, it is clear that a Whiteheadian outlook is required if a collaborative culture is to be achieved. Staff must be valued, recognized as professionals and assumed to want to do their best for the children they teach. This does not, of course, mean colleagues are simply left to their own devices. As we saw in Chapter 1, schools serious about quality have in place mechanisms for monitoring staff performance and pupil achievement. Schools in which a positive ethos is instantly recognizable are likely to have in place sensible structures, procedures and monitoring, balanced with a good deal of individual autonomy for both staff and students.

School culture and effectiveness

In 1993 a report was produced for the Department for Education on effective school management. Twenty-four secondary schools were involved in the survey and the staff in those schools recognized the following as contributing to effective management practice which helped to generate a positive school ethos:

- students play an active part in the life of the school and there are high expectations of them in terms of behaviour and achievement;
- complacency among staff is actively discouraged in favour of a questioning, critical attitude;
- there is an open atmosphere; staff respect one another and talk freely about professional matters;
- staff are involved in developing the school's aims and policies;
- all staff have a clear understanding of the school's vision;
- the head is accessible to staff and has a consultative 'listening' style;
- the head praises staff and celebrates their achievements;

- the SMT delegate tasks to develop and empower staff but also monitor performance;
- working parties operate to reach decisions and write policies;
- struggling staff are supported;
- staff feel valued and their views are taken seriously;
- professional development for all staff is encouraged;
- many decisions are made collaboratively.

This is not the complete list, but the points above are useful in guiding us to a conclusion regarding effective school cultures. A good summary is provided by Ainscow (1994) who suggests that 'the type of school cultures most supportive of school improvement efforts are those that are collaborative, have high expectations for both students and staff, exhibit a consensus of values, and support an orderly and secure environment'. Many of these features are to be found in schools aiming for a collaborative model of organization. While the existence of these features will not be a guarantee that *all* staff in schools displaying them will be motivated, involved and productive, it is more likely that a *critical mass* of the staff will be.

Further evidence of effective school cultures was provided by Sammons *et al.* (1995). They were commissioned by OFSTED to undertake a review of international school effectiveness literature, particularly from the United Kingdom, North America and the Netherlands. They were asked to assess whether or not, despite very different approaches to education in different countries, successful schools had common distinctive features. They came up with eleven key characteristics found in effective schools in all the countries studied:

- professional leadership which encourages participation;
- shared vision and goals generated by collegiality and collaboration;
- an orderly learning environment;
- a focus on achievement;
- purposeful teaching;
- high expectations;
- positive reinforcement;
- effective monitoring of progress;
- active involvement of pupils;
- parental involvement;
- a strong emphasis on staff development.

Once again, the collaborative culture is in evidence, suggesting that this approach is the most likely to generate success in secondary schools. In management literature the collaborative culture is associated with collegial models of management.

Collegiality

> Collegial models assume that organisations determine policy and make decisions through a process of discussion leading to consensus. Power is shared among some or all members of the organization who are thought to have a mutual understanding about the objectives of the institution. (Bush 1994)

Middle managers working in schools which have developed such an approach have the advantage that most colleagues in their teams are likely to be receptive to team work, sharing ideas and working towards agreed goals. This does not, however, mean that *all* colleagues will be. Middle managers not working in schools with a collaborative/collegiate culture may find it more difficult to involve their teams in new ways of working, but changing 'the way we do things around here' is possible. How managers can begin to support colleagues in changing their practice is a theme covered in Chapter 4.

Case studies

Below are two extracts from articles about real head teachers. Read each one and then reflect on the questions that follow.

Study 1

In 1996 *The Ridings School* in Halifax hit the national headlines as 'the school from hell'. So serious were its problems that the school was temporarily closed and reopened under the leadership of Peter Clarke, seconded from a local GM school, and Anna White. Mrs White subsequently became head teacher of *The Ridings*, which was removed from special measures in 1998. In an interview in the *Evening Courier*, the local newspaper, Mrs White made the following statements in response to a question about the government's idea of creating a team of 'super heads' to take over the running of groups of schools:

> I am not convinced that the idea of super heads running groups of schools has been fully thought out. Super schools are created not by super heads, but by super staff and students working together with a shared sense of self worth and vision. I have never thought that any one individual could swoop in and sort out the troubles of a school. Of course we can provide a fresh vision and new ideas. We can set targets and lead by example but we must, above all, engender a

shared sense of purpose and this can only be done by ensuring that all involved work as a team to achieve their goals. (*Halifax Evening Courier*)

Reflection

- What type of organizational culture is Anna White clearly in favour of?
- Look back to Chapter 1 and consider Peter Clarke's words about the role of middle managers. Are his views in harmony with those of Anna White?
- How would the views expressed by Mrs White affect staff morale?
- Consider why working for a head teacher who believed in the collaborative culture might be better for a middle manager than working for a head who favoured some other culture.

Study 2

Joan Sallis has outlined the case of a head teacher who tried to impose a new culture on his school and lost much respect in the process. We take up the story from when Dr X had been appointed as head teacher.

Passionate about achievement, he was also very much aware of the problems of the inner city and totally committed to comprehensive education. Nevertheless, he was shaken to find the commitment to mixed ability teaching in all subjects at the school was total and uncompromising. Still, he kept an open mind until he had been in the school for six months. After studying the pattern of achievement in detail against all the information he could get about ability levels, he became convinced that the school was doing a disservice to all students and announced, just like that, that from September there would be setting throughout the school in all subjects.

The staff were outraged that such a decision was even contemplated and furious that it should have been announced without consultation. There was talk of industrial action. The head said it was an internal management matter, as the arrangement of classes and delivery of the curriculum always had been. The governors took advice on this and were told that, although technically the head had a case, it was absurd to think that so fundamental and wholesale a change, likely to have a big impact among staff, parents and community, could be imposed by either governing body or head unilaterally. It must be a shared decision.

This argument raged for a while, but after a time Dr. X became more realistic and accepted that he could not carry this change with the staff unless he had powerful support from governors. He announced that there would be a period of consultation and discussion before decisions were taken. (*Managing Schools Today*, September 1997)

Reflection

- What kind of culture seems to have existed before Dr X became head teacher?
- What management style did Dr X display when he announced that mixed ability teaching was to end?
- What would have been the effect on staff morale of this approach?
- Which school culture allows practices to change without the kind of confrontation seen in this example?
- How should Dr X have handled this situation?
- What are the lessons for middle managers?

Summary

Institutions of all kinds display different cultures or 'ways of doing things' and schools are no exception. In recent years, a range of school cultures has been identified by researchers and there is now a considerable body of evidence indicating that secondary schools which adopt a collegiate approach to management are the most effective. This style is now being encouraged in management literature as a means of improving school effectiveness and there are cases on record of this approach being employed to assist in turning round failing schools.

A collegiate approach is likely to generate a collaborative ethos, characterized by a clear vision, staff involvement in decision-making and a culture of critical reflection, learning from peers and professional development. Teachers working in a collaborative culture are likely to have considerable autonomy, flexibility and responsibility, within a framework of monitoring and evaluation of their performance. There is also likely to be much discussion about how to improve teaching and learning and the students themselves will probably be involved in this.

To be effective in such cultures middle managers need to be good team players, supportive, self-critical, reflective and not frightened by the prospect of empowering colleagues in their teams. They will not be concerned by status, hierarchy and the kind of power that comes from rigid job descriptions. They will be good at delegating and will take pride in allowing others in their team to flower and grow. Middle managers not working in schools characterized by collaborative features can still achieve a great deal of collegiality within their own teams. However, while some staff not used to working collegially will rise to the challenge, others may be reluctant and fearful and will need careful nurturing away from the state of dependency in which they have been allowed to exist.

CHAPTER FOUR

Getting the Best out of People

Introduction

When I was being trained as a teacher in the late 1970s a lot of time was devoted to discussing what was the best approach to educating young people. One school of thought was that young people should be seen as empty pots, waiting to be filled with knowledge which we, the teachers, defined as valuable. Our level of education and experience, so the argument went, provided us with the necessary authority to decide what was best for the pupils in our care. This was challenged by those who saw children as being more like delicate plants which, when provided with the right environment, would develop naturally to reveal their full beauty. Too much shaping and pruning, it was argued, would hinder development. What was needed was stimulation not control.

These debates and discussions were over-simplified and polarized into what became seen in the media as a choice between 'traditional' and 'progressive' teaching methods and what teachers in some schools saw as a choice between 'passive' and 'active' learning. The legislative changes of the last twenty years, especially the introduction of the national curriculum and school inspection, have removed the likelihood of teachers being able to maintain either of the extreme and simplified positions outlined above. Good practice in the classroom involves combining both approaches. What successful teachers are able to do, of course, is differentiate between classes and individuals within classes in terms of the balance of passivity and activity required for effective learning to occur.

There are very real similarities between successful teaching, which enables children to develop, and effective management, which enables members of a team to improve their skills and potential. While team leaders in school are usually well aware of the need to differentiate when planning lessons in order to help all pupils to progress, they do not always apply the same logic to the nurturing of people in their teams. Indeed, there are still some 'authoritarian' managers who treat junior colleagues rather like empty pots and some 'laissez-faire' managers who imagine that people in their teams will magically develop if they are simply left alone to do so.

Middle managers should see helping colleagues to develop professionally as a duty. Effective teachers assess children in order to plan their learning programmes, and good managers think carefully about the needs of their team members in order to help them develop their skills and abilities. Clearly, a newly qualified teacher entering a department will have quite different needs to a very experienced teacher who has signalled a desire to retire early. It is important for middle managers not just to realize this but to act upon it. Before they can do this, however, team leaders must develop an understanding of what motivates people and must strive to develop good practice in their handling of colleagues, just as teachers must develop good classroom organization and discipline before they can turn their attention to differentiation.

What motivates people?

Psychologists and sociologists have produced many theories that attempt to explain what motivates people in work. Over the years various companies have experimented with altering the working environment, providing financial rewards for increases in productivity and using a range of sticks and carrots in order to get the best out of their employees. In education, the production of performance tables based on national tests and exam results has made target setting for schools possible and it seems likely that some kind of performance related pay will be introduced into education in the near future. Of course, it is possible that regular appraisal of teachers and target setting will improve results in areas that are easily measured. However, this approach does not always generate a sense of loyalty to a school and can, in fact, be counter-productive if teachers cease to give time to areas of school life which are not so easily measured. Middle managers need to make use of appraisal and targets (see Chapter 10) but there is much else that can be done to motivate colleagues.

In the commercial world companies have come to appreciate the importance of developing loyalty in their workers. Through initiatives such as *Investors in People* they have attempted to organize themselves in ways which show that their human resources are valued. Increasingly, companies have a *mission statement* and employees are encouraged to share the company's *vision* and help the organization move towards achieving its goals. Schools, also, are beginning to use these techniques as a way of helping to create a clear and shared sense of purpose. It is obvious that teachers are the most important resource in schools and their commitment is vital to the success of any improvement initiatives.

> Of all the resources at the disposal of an organisation it is only people who can grow and develop and be motivated to achieve certain desired ends. The attaining of targets is in their hands and it is the way people are managed ... which is at the heart of human resource management ... and optimum management. (Riches and Morgan 1989)

It is essential, therefore, to engage teachers actively in the shaping of the school and ensure that they feel valued and in possession of high levels of skill. As indicated in Chapters 2 and 3 democratic leadership styles and collaborative school cultures are more likely to generate success and commitment from most teachers than other approaches. This can partly be explained by the ideas of Abraham Maslow.

Maslow produced a theory of motivation that sought to go beyond financial and environmental considerations when explaining employee behaviour. This theory, conceived in the 1950s, still has much to commend it and certainly seems to explain why so many teachers work as hard as they do with seemingly little financial reward. According to Maslow there are various needs that humans have to satisfy and these should be seen as a hierarchy. More basic or low-level needs, he argued, must be satisfied before a higher need becomes important (see Figure 4.1). The lowest order needs are physiological ones: hunger, thirst and warmth. In most cases, people at work have already satisfied these needs through having money to pay for them. Regarding safety needs, Maslow argues that, in today's society, these only act as motivators at times of crisis that threaten safety or life, such as fire, natural catastrophes, crime waves and other emergency situations. Social needs, however, do act as motivators in the workplace as most people need to feel they *belong*. Most people don't just go to work to put in the hours so that they can earn enough money to enjoy the time they are not at work. If the work satisfies social needs, the next stage in the hierarchy is that of esteem needs. To have self-esteem you need to feel a sense of achievement in what you do and to gain the respect of those you work with; from self-esteem stem feelings of self-confidence and self-worth. According to Maslow *self-actualization* is the most developed level, and not all humans will manage to reach it. In my experience self-actualization, the need for self-development and realizing one's potential, is certainly what drives many teachers. It is not possible to generalize, of course, but so many teachers I meet are not overly materialistic and often seem more motivated by a

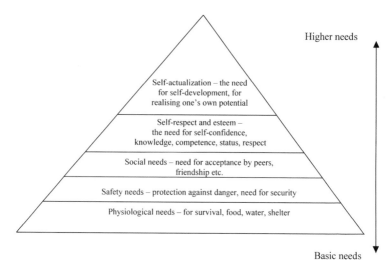

Figure 4.1   Maslow's Hierarchy of Needs

genuine desire to achieve their full potential and that of their pupils than by financial rewards.

Motivating others through good practice

Maslow's hierarchy shows us that people are motivated by a range of needs and may be motivated in different ways at different stages of their life. However, the importance Maslow places on higher level needs provides valuable insights into people's motivation and gives us a useful starting point for some general rules on good practice for managers. If Maslow's contention that people are driven by the desire for acceptance by peers, self-respect and self-actualization is correct then managers would be wise to reflect on their behaviour towards colleagues in terms of how it affects their feelings of acceptance, their self-respect and their opportunity for self-actualization. Listening to teachers complaining about the way they have been treated by managers adds weight to Maslow's theory and also to the importance of creating collaborative school cultures (discussed in Chapter 3).

The following statements apply to most, though not all, teachers I have met and worked with.

- Teachers like to be consulted about what they have to do – just being told what to do does not generate feelings of *ownership* for a particular policy.

- Teachers appreciate managers who are willing to listen – feeling that your views are of no significance is demotivating.
- Teachers appreciate being seen as valuable individuals with specialist skills – being seen as a mere cog in the machine, easily replaced by other cogs, does not build self-esteem.
- Teachers respond to sensitive managers – heavy-handed use of authority is often counter-productive.
- Teachers perform better when they enjoy their work and feel relaxed – managers who can spread good cheer and empower teachers will be helping to motivate them.
- Teachers whose successes are recognized become more successful and more motivated – praise for teachers is as important as praise for their pupils.

From these statements it is not difficult to arrive at some general, though very important pointers on good practice for middle managers.

1. Spend time getting to know the people in your team and then support them

When you become a middle manager it is worth spending time getting to know the people for whom you have a management responsibility. Your knowledge of the people in your team will help you to manage situations more easily, for example by being able to anticipate people's likely reactions to new ideas. As you get to know people you will become concerned for their welfare and as this begins to show it is likely to bring you greater loyalty than managers who stand aloof. Showing that you are interested in colleagues as people and as professionals will encourage the members of your team to offer you the support that you will need to do your job effectively.

Getting to know colleagues is sure to make you want to help them to do their best and this will make you a better manager. The head of department who tries to support team members who are looking under the weather, by relieving them for ten minutes during a lesson or taking a cover lesson they have been put down for, will not only help to prevent them 'going under' (thus saving work) but will also earn goodwill which is likely to be repaid many times over. This makes management sense, but the desire to support comes also from a genuine wish to help colleagues you have taken the time to get to know.

2. Communicate clearly with your team and don't be frightened by debate
It is important that people in your team do not feel they are being kept in the dark about important new developments. Talk to colleagues about any plans or schemes and ask for their ideas. Remember that any initiatives

you think up are unlikely to succeed without the support of a *critical mass* of team members. Always explain things clearly. People are more likely to cooperate if they know what they are supposed to be doing. If you are putting in place a policy generated externally, for example responding to new legislation, or initiated by senior managers, involve your team as much as possible in deciding *how* the scheme will operate in your area.

A sense of ownership is really important if a new initiative is to succeed. Your team should not just be briefed about it but should have the chance to talk it through in a free and open exchange of views. This can act as a real safety valve, allowing people to share their worries and concerns. When there is no dialogue, people will be more likely to begin muttering in small groups and in these circumstances dissatisfaction can soon take hold.

3. Make decisions!

While it is important to consult people in your team and to keep them informed about important developments it is not necessary to involve all team members in every decision that has to be made. One of your responsibilities as a manager is to shield colleagues from trivia and minutiae so that they are free to devote their energies to the children in their classrooms. Colleagues would, quite rightly, be annoyed if you allocated teaching groups without consultation but there is nothing to be gained in consulting your team about whether or not to order another box of blackboard chalk!

Those decisions that require time, thought and consultation will still need resolution and expecting colleagues to attend many long meetings is unrealistic. Taking the time to make a good decision is one thing – being indecisive is quite another and is fatal if you want to be an effective manager. Of course, involving people in making important decisions is good and getting people *on side* will increase the likelihood of success. However, not all decisions can be democratic and it is not always possible to get everyone in your team to be enthusiastic about every initiative. Finally, if you realize that a decision you made was wrong don't be afraid to admit it. Managers who are open about their mistakes (unless mistakes are made all the time) earn more respect than those who insist on pushing ahead with flawed plans.

4. Display self-control and be positive

Good managers calmly find ways to solve problems and they do not make mountains out of molehills. Respect is more likely to be gained by being calm when things go wrong than by creating anxiety in others by exaggerating the importance of small mistakes they have made. You will soon lose the respect of colleagues if you constantly challenge them over minor matters and this will make tackling major issues more difficult. There is nothing constructive in interrogating members of your team about a missing pencil sharpener! However, if stock control is an issue of concern then it can be put on the agenda for a team meeting so that all can have their say. I have encountered some middle managers so obsessed with insignificant day-to-day matters that they never properly address the really important issues. Indeed, over-attention to detail can be a method employed, perhaps unconsciously, to avoid having to face more difficult decisions and can sometimes be a sign that the manager in question is suffering serious stress. Remember, as a manager you will never reach the hilltop if you allow yourself to get bogged down in the mud in the valley.

5. Lead by example

You cannot expect other people to do what you are not able or prepared to do yourself. As a team leader you should set a high standard in the amount and the quality of the work you do and in your general attitude to your pupils. You cannot expect to grumble about your workload and show cynicism for whole-school initiatives and then expect people in your team enthusiastically to embrace new ideas you have. You cannot allocate yourself all the higher ability classes and then complain to colleagues about the behaviour or results of their groups. In short, you have to lead from the front.

Some managers find it difficult to admit their own weaknesses. It is vital that you share your classroom failures as well as your successes with your team if you expect them to be open with you about their weaknesses. Creating a genuinely collaborative team ethos requires openness and critical self-reflection from everyone; this is much more likely to be achieved if the team leader makes it clear that they understand that nobody can be excellent at everything. This, of course, is not an excuse for poor performance, but the foundation stones of a team culture that enables all members to improve by learning from, and supporting, one another.

6. Be considerate and fair

The maxim 'treat other people as you would wish to be treated yourself' is an important one for middle managers. This means more than simply being pleasant and friendly towards others, it means thinking about the impact your actions will have on their self-esteem and motivation. It also means not forgetting that members of your team also have responsibilities in other areas of school and are entitled to a family life. You cannot expect people to drop what they are doing to fit into your plans just because you are the team leader. Consult your colleagues before you arrange a trip or team activity so that you can choose a time and date which suits the majority. If you are fair with your team you will get more out of them and when there is a genuine crisis which requires them to change their plans at short notice, they are more likely to try and help you out.

One of the ways in which fairness becomes transparent is in the allocation of groups, rooms and duties to team members. It is very important that the criteria for group and room allocation are clear to everyone. A member of staff historically being allocated particular groups and rooms is not of itself a good reason for continuing the practice. It is a middle manager's duty to ensure that younger colleagues are nurtured and developed in terms of the range of groups and subjects they teach and that more senior colleagues experience their fair share of the 'challenging' groups.

7. Listen to people

The ability to listen carefully and, when necessary, sympathetically is an important skill for any team leader. Middle managers should be willing to listen properly to the concerns of individuals in their teams and need to be accessible. This does not mean dropping everything at the precise moment someone mentions something to you; if necessary arrange another time that suits you both. It is important to remember when arranging such meetings that things usually take longer to discuss than you (or they) estimate they will. Being willing to give up time to help people is an important aspect of management responsibility and should not be regarded as a burden, even though it will take you away from other aspects of your role. You should regard time spent listening as a good investment as it really can help you to nip problems in the bud, and by supporting colleagues through difficult times you are helping to nurture the collaborative and supportive culture which will allow your team to flourish.

Middle managers should also be skilled in assessing the mood of a meeting, by listening carefully to what is being said. The democratic leader should not expect always to have the last word. When people are talking they should be given your full attention and when they have finished their contribution it is useful to sum up their ideas to make sure you have grasped fully what they have said. When new ideas are being proposed people's initial response can often be to focus on the negatives. This is understandable, as people are generally cautious when it comes to change, not least because extra work is likely to be involved. Be patient and allow people their say. It is amazing how soon a real debate will begin and, if the new idea is a good one, how quickly the proposals will be embraced. Trying to force your ideas on people without debate is counter-productive and undermines collaboration and trust.

8. Spread good cheer!

I had the pleasure of working for a head teacher who included 'the ability to spread good cheer' as an essential quality on selection criteria sheets sent to prospective candidates for management posts in the school. The importance of this should never be under-estimated. In far too many staff rooms you will find disgruntled middle managers being negative and cynical. No doubt individual cynics will have their personal reasons for their lack of enthusiasm, but they are being unprofessional and failing in their duties as managers through their actions. Keeping up staff morale is a central role of middle managers and it can be achieved in quite small, but very significant, ways.

Always give credit where it is due and always give praise and thanks when it is deserved. Often this will be done in a one-to-one situation but praising individuals in the presence of others (at a department meeting or a staff briefing) should occur when colleagues have special achievements worthy of sharing. Take pride in announcing what people in your team have achieved and never see their successes as a threat to your status. Managers should be judged, at least in part, by what they have allowed and encouraged those in their teams to achieve. It is especially important to praise newly qualified teachers in the presence of a third party as you are trying to build their confidence and socialize them into the supportive culture of your team.

Praise, thanks and attention provide what are called *positive strokes* and these help to build up morale and confidence. We all want to be appreciated and valued but, sadly, it often feels like the media and government have little that is positive to say about teachers. This can undermine morale and self-confidence and makes it all the more difficult to motivate staff. It is true that success breeds success and it is also true that negative talk can create failure or at least sap enthusiasm. By spreading good cheer and publicizing achievement middle managers help to keep up the morale of their teams and help individuals to feel valued and appreciated.

With the above foundation stones of good practice in place it will be easier to handle difficult issues which you encounter (such as the poor performance of a colleague) and to consider the individual development needs of members of your team.

Situational leadership

In Chapter 2 it was suggested that a democratic approach to management in education was desirable and in Chapter 3 empowerment and autonomy for colleagues was encouraged. However, not *all* teachers respond to the good practice of democratic management and not *all* teachers are capable of acting autonomously. This is where situational leadership becomes important as a way of dealing with colleagues with different levels of professional competence.

Schools that have embraced a *total quality management* approach regard teachers as internal clients and, therefore, meeting their development needs is a natural function of the organization. In all schools helping teachers to develop and improve their skills is obviously central to improving the achievement of pupils. While being fair and consistent with all members of your team it is important to remember that 'there is nothing so unequal as the equal treatment of unequals' (Blanchard 1994). Teachers know this to be true in meeting the needs of the pupils they teach; it is also true for managers addressing the professional development needs of people in their teams.

Effective managers, therefore, need to be flexible in the management styles they use (even if their ideal style is democratic) depending on the individuals they are dealing with. The choice of style used will depend on an assessment of the needs of the individual concerned. This assessment may be formal through, say, appraisal (see Chapter 10) but is more likely to be instinctive, based on day-to-day observation and discussion with colleagues. A collaborative culture makes it much easier for a manager to slip naturally between the situational leadership styles outlined in Table 4.1.

All of these styles have their uses for middle managers and experienced team leaders move so easily between them that individuals on the receiving end are often unaware of different approaches being used with different team members. If they are aware they are rarely disgruntled by it, as skilful managers are operating within a culture of trust and support which they have created. Indeed, in an effective team it will not just be

Directing	*Coaching*	*Supporting*	*Delegating*
The leader provides very clear and specific direction and closely monitors results achieved	The leader directs and supervises but also explains decisions, encourages suggestions and supports progress	The leader facilitates and supports team members in decision-making and accomplishing tasks	The leader delegates responsibility for decision-making and task completion to team members

Table 4.1 Situational leadership styles

the team leader who is using these styles but all colleagues, as they support each other.

A consideration of these four styles reveals a balance between directive behaviour and supportive behaviour. Directive behaviour involves telling people what to do, how to do it, when to do it, and then monitoring performance. Supportive behaviour involves listening to people, providing support and encouragement, and facilitating involvement in decision-making. Different circumstances and different individuals require different combinations of directive and supportive behaviour and middle managers will need to use careful judgements when considering the best approach to adopt. In general though the styles can be applied to team members as shown in Table 4.2.

Typically, then, a directing style would be used when inducting new teachers into certain departmental procedures. A coaching style might be used with colleagues who have been identified as under-performing in some aspect of their work. A supporting style is the style that is likely to be used most often and is in harmony with a democratic approach to management. Delegation can be used with experienced and committed colleagues and is especially useful for providing ambitious and competent teachers with experiences that might help them gain promotion to management posts. However, it is important to remember that people's level of competence and commitment can vary with different aspects of their jobs. It is quite possible, for example, to find very competent and committed teachers who nevertheless lack well developed IT skills and may need coaching or even directing in this area. Equally, newly qualified teachers may bring high levels of IT skills into a department, even though they need directing in departmental procedures.

Team leaders are likely to find themselves managing people other than teachers, in particular student teachers, non-teaching assistants and

Style	Characteristics of team member
Directing	Low level of competence but high level of commitment
Coaching	Basic level of competence but low level of commitment
Supporting	High level of competence but variable level of commitment
Delegating	High level of competence and high level of commitment

Table 4.2   Situational style and characteristics of team member

technicians. While the same situational leadership styles can be applied it is very important to remember that people who have not been through teacher training may require much more directing and coaching. Middle managers must not be reluctant to direct non-teaching colleagues; in my experience they are keen to do the best they can for the pupils they support and welcome clear guidance and direction, especially when they are new to their role. Again, time spent with non-teaching team members should be regarded as an investment that will pay dividends in the future.

Middle managers who have to deal with members of their teams who are encountering difficulties usually find this the most stressful and difficult aspect of their work. Helping colleagues to improve their performance is certainly a management challenge. However, struggling colleagues cannot be ignored and middle managers who fail to address their development needs let down not just the struggling colleague but the children in their care. The needs of the vast majority of teachers can be met by appropriate support from their team leader. However, in situations where there are serious weaknesses, it is vital to involve senior managers in deciding on the best way to handle such colleagues (see Chapter 10).

Some thoughts on coaching

Managers in school should also be successful teachers. They have well-developed skills and competencies worth sharing with less experienced colleagues and teachers undergoing initial training. Good managers share their skills in the hope that members of their team can become as effective or more effective in the classroom than they are. They also facilitate opportunities for other colleagues in their teams to share good practice, with continuously improving performance being a central aim.

Coaching involves helping another person to develop their skills and knowledge: 'passing on your experience to someone else rather as masters did to apprentices in the past. It should be a rewarding experience for both the coach and the learner; if it is not, then the coaching is not being effective' (Thomson 1998).

Coaching is time-consuming and it requires paying attention to:
- the learner's precise needs;
- the learner's preferred learning style;
- developing the learning skills of the learner.

Teachers generally make good coaches as they are used to using coaching skills with the children they teach. Middle managers need not do all the coaching themselves. It is good experience for other colleagues to undertake coaching and helps to develop their communication skills and self-confidence. As with teaching and management there is no single coaching style for all situations. A careful analysis of a range of factors will determine the style adopted. A protective, kindly and reassuring approach might be used with a teacher who lacks confidence whereas a tougher and more demanding style might be employed on a capable but lazy colleague. Always try and think through what the consequences of choosing a particular style will be. Sometimes, several people have similar needs and can be coached together. In fact, many heads of department regularly use departmental meetings as opportunities for particular colleagues to coach the rest of the team.

Case studies

The following comments, made to me by different teachers over the years, illustrate just how motivational Maslow's notion of 'higher needs' can be.

Case 1
'I am absolutely determined to get this class through with brilliant grades. Bob trusted me with "A" level work and I will give extra lessons every lunch hour if necessary to prove that I am up to it.' (English teacher in her second year of teaching)

Case 2
'I know it's a lot of money, but I'm doing this for myself. If school can't pay the fees I will pay them. I've told myself for years that once my children are old enough I'll study for a Masters and that's what I'm determined to do.' (Middle-aged applicant for M.Ed degree)

Case 3
'I am more interested in gaining this post for the challenge than the money. A few hundred pounds won't make much difference to my life-style; I just feel ready for a change, a new challenge, a different role. I'm very happy at this school and I know I'm respected but I feel as if I've not yet achieved my full potential – and I don't want to regret that later in life.' (Colleague discussing applying for a senior teacher post in a new school)

> **Case 4**
>
> 'I felt really deflated, as if he didn't trust me. I know I'm capable of producing a brilliant magazine and the kids are so keen. He kept saying I needed more experience before starting something so major and he kept going on about the time and effort needed. Surely I'm the best judge of how much time I can give and I really wanted to prove I could handle a whole-school initiative.' (Teacher with two years, experience, after speaking to her head of department about taking on responsibility for the school magazine)

Reflection

There is much to be learnt from these examples. As a middle manager in school I met many colleagues who worked very hard indeed in response to being given a responsibility that boosted their self-confidence. Often the responsibility they had been given was unpaid, but the effect it had on their self-esteem was tremendous. Making people feel trusted, skilled and valued are strong motivators indeed. I well remember the first time I was invited, as a head of department, to provide input at a regional conference. I worked extremely hard to make sure that the session I had been trusted with went well, even though I was not being paid for my efforts and the conference was on a Saturday!

Market research indicates that about half the teachers undertaking part-time study towards a higher degree pay their own fees. Of course, many of them feel that gaining such a qualification will improve their chances of promotion but for others the desire for self-actualization is what drives them. Likewise, many teachers who take on promoted posts do so as much for self-development as for the small financial reward that is so often involved. Many people enter teaching from a genuine desire, a calling, to work with young people. These teachers represent a significant proportion of the profession and, when managed effectively, show great motivation.

Middle managers must help members of their team to develop. It is very demotivating and deskilling (as in Case 4) to reject the suggestions of team members without discussion and to undermine their hopes and plans. If their desires are unreasonable or genuinely incompatible with the vision of the school or the needs of your area then careful handling is required so that they can be let down gently. Likewise, if you have good reason to think a team member is being over-ambitious then think of ways in which they can be supported or their plans can be modified, rather than simply rejecting them. Always try and support team members in what they want to do. Take pride in their achievements and be grateful that they are so highly motivated. Dealing with disillusioned and disgruntled colleagues is far more challenging than supporting and empowering the enthusiastic.

Summary

The Teacher Training Agency's *National Standards for Subject Leaders* includes the ability to 'deal sensitively with people, recognising individual needs and take account of these in securing a consistent team approach to raising achievement' (TTA 1998) as a skill required of middle managers. This involves the flexible use of directing, coaching, supporting and delegating with team members, depending on the particular individuals and the specific issues being dealt with. Successful middle managers move between styles with sensitivity and tact, so as to help the professional development of their colleagues.

The successful application of these four styles occurs most successfully when a team ethos of support, collaboration and openness has been achieved. Such a culture is most likely to be created by managers who show a genuine interest in team members, keep people informed and seek their opinions, stay calm and remain positive, are fair, lead by example, smile and praise and publicly and sincerely celebrate the successes of team members.

Adair (1997) sums up the approach required very neatly:

The six most important words...
'I admit I made a mistake.'

The five most important words...
'I am proud of you.'

The four most important words...
'What is your opinion?'

The three most important words...
'If you please.'

The two most important words...
'Thank you.'

The one most important word...
'We.'

And the last, least important word...
'I.'

CHAPTER FIVE

Building Your Team

Introduction

Many teams exist in the average secondary school. Some teams are permanent, for example departments, faculties, year teams and the SMT, although membership changes as a result of staff being promoted, staff retiring or internal restructuring. Other teams are temporary, for example working groups established to write a particular policy document or plan a school production. Some teams operate very formally, for example governing bodies, whereas other teams can be quite informal, a group of colleagues who have taken on responsibility for organizing staff social events, for instance. Some teams have limited membership, for example the SMT usually comprises the head, deputies and senior teachers only, whereas other teams offer open access, for instance a working party on behaviour. Membership of some teams is voluntary but membership of other teams is contractual. In secondary schools most teachers belong to at least two teams, a subject team and a pastoral team.

Some teams are much more effective than others. Indeed, it would be fair to conclude that many teams are not really teams at all but simply groups of people placed together because they teach the same subject or are responsible for classes containing pupils of the same age group, for example. In such groups the activities of individuals frequently limit, rather than enhance, the effectiveness of the whole. There may be jealousies between members, information suppressed and cooperation withheld because members see themselves as being in competition with each other. Alternatively, there may be apathy and indifference resulting from a lack of team vision or sense of direction.

A major challenge for middle managers is to transform a group of people they have responsibility for, lumped together under some functional umbrella, into a successful team. Teams thrive best in collaborative cultures (see Chapter 3) and in situations where the team leader is committed to the development of each individual (see Chapter

4). Even then, there is still much effort and skill needed in creating and maintaining a genuine team. Where really effective teams do exist, the support which team members receive from each other, the rapport that exists and the sense of working for common goals is very powerful. In fact, a successful team becomes very visible to others working in the school and it is not unusual for pupils to notice and comment upon this. It is a real achievement indeed when the atmosphere generated by a successful team is absorbed by pupils and begins to influence their behaviour.

What makes a group of people a team?

1. Vision and sense of direction

Having shared goals is the first thing that distinguishes groups from teams. This is why it is so important that the team leader has a clear sense of direction. This should be provided partly by the vision or mission of the school, with the team leader's job being to translate the vision into something meaningful at team level. A clear sense of direction will also come from the team leader being certain about what their team is uniquely contributing to the education of young people. If you are in charge of History then what is your vision of excellent History teaching? What can your subject uniquely contribute to the education of young people? If you are a year head what is your vision of successful pastoral care? What uniquely can form teachers contribute to the education of young people? These question are fundamental and need to be discussed and answers agreed upon by team members in order to provide both a sense of direction and an under-pinning philosophy to the work of the team.

2. The behaviour of the team leader

It is important that leaders are able to give their teams space for development, that they can listen to the views of others and can encourage participation. Team leaders should encourage collegiality and adopt a democratic style of leadership. They must be self-critical and committed to the idea that their authority comes more from their behaviour and the example they set than from their title. Team leaders will want individuals in their team to progress and develop and will be skilful at directing, coaching, supporting and delegating, as appropriate. The team leader will be visible and accessible and will strive to build the self-esteem of all team members.

3. The extent to which people pull together

A team exists if members embrace the team vision and work together to achieve it. The result is team members becoming interdependent, with particular strengths of individuals recognized and used to the benefit of the whole team and the pupils. Team members also support each other and just as the leader looks for opportunities to develop each member so members look for opportunities to develop other members and the team leader. This does not mean that there are never any disagreements. Open debate is encouraged and is one of the things that helps to clarify team values and the direction the team is going in. Team successes are celebrated publicly as are the achievements of individual team members. It is not unusual to hear laughter coming from meetings of successful teams. This indicates a relaxed rapport has been achieved and is in no way at odds with a team's serious purpose.

4. Open lines of communication

Team members talk to each other about issues and there is an atmosphere in which positive and negative feedback can be given. People are open-minded to other people's arguments and new ideas are encouraged and debated. Individual team members are assertive but not aggressive and conflicting viewpoints are seen as normal. Indeed, lively debate is seen as a constructive feature of decision-making. While lines of communication are open there are also clear procedures for holding meetings and making decisions.

5. Regular reviews of progress

Teams are not frightened of reviewing progress. Successes are celebrated and failures are analysed so as to build on good practice and avoid repeating mistakes. All team members are involved in development planning and target setting.

An effective team combines creativity and energy to produce an output greater than the sum of its parts – this is known as *synergy*. You may have experienced synergy as part of a team putting on a public performance such as a show or maybe during an OFSTED inspection. What probably sticks in your mind is the real sense of working together for a common goal. Synergy is what good team leaders try and create in the everyday work of their teams.

A quick mental checklist for making appraisals of team functioning is provided by Hardingham (1995) using the acronym PERFORM. This has been modified to suit a school context in Figure 5.1.

Productivity	Is the team getting enough done? Is there evidence that the work being done is raising pupil achievement?
Empathy	Do the team members feel comfortable with one another? Do they encourage one another to succeed?
Roles and goals	Do they know what they're supposed to be doing?
Flexibility	Are they open to outside influence, willing regularly to review roles and keen to innovate?
Openness	Do they say what they think? Are meetings lively with plenty of debate?
Recognition	Do they praise one another and publicize achievement?
Morale	Do people want to be in this team? Do team members spread good cheer?
	Common indicators of problems in these areas are:
Productivity	A team leader in a bad temper; performance targets not met
Empathy	No coffee at team meetings; tension between members
Roles and goals	Puzzled faces in meetings; unfinished tasks
Flexibility	Annoyed outsiders talking about the 'fortress mentality'; failure to embrace new ideas; complacency
Openness	Silence in meetings
Recognition	Backbiting; jealousy; splinter groups
Morale	No laughter at meetings; everyone looking for new jobs; people clock-watch and religiously stick to 1265 hours and contractual duties

Figure 5.1   Effective team checklist

The team life-cycle

As well as understanding the difference between a team and a group, it is useful to understand the different stages that teams go through as they develop. Research has shown that these stages are fairly predictable.

Stage 1 - Forming

At this stage the newly created team is a group of people who are getting the measure of each other. They are concerned with 'who fits where'. Group members may exhibit self-conscious politeness, embarrassment, stilted communication or false enthusiasm.

Stage 2 – Storming

At this stage team members' different personalities and approaches to work can begin to clash. There is concern over 'how we work together' and a certain amount of 'juggling for position'. Group members may come into conflict and there is likely to be heated debate and discussion. Nevertheless, things begin to be achieved.

Stage 3 – Norming

At this stage the 'rules of the game' become clear and the members of the team begin to exhibit group behaviour. Goals are focused on effectively and a more relaxed and purposeful atmosphere emerges.

Stage 4 – Performing

The team now settles into a comfortable way of working and decisions and agreements are reached more easily. There is a feeling of confidence and achievement, with individuals in the team clear about roles and responsibilities.

With some teams in school these stages are easily recognized. Working parties, formed with a specific goal in mind, often follow this pattern. For established subject or year teams the cycle can be iterative, with teams switching between stages as they encounter new issues to resolve. In some ways the organization of schools around the academic year, with the long summer break, encourages teams to make a fresh start each September, especially as there are usually some newly appointed colleagues joining teams at this point. It is very important that middle managers create opportunities for newcomers to contribute to team activity so that norming is accomplished quickly. Sadly, some teams never seem to develop beyond the storming stage.

Newly appointed middle managers often feel quite vulnerable when taking over an established team. A team culture or ethos will already exist and some members will feel anxious and irritated by the prospect of the inevitable forming, storming and norming that will occur. New managers are likely to be compared with the team leaders they replace as new roles and ways of working evolve, making it a stressful time. It is important that new team leaders behave with tact and integrity and do not fall into the trap of feeling they have to dominate others in order to prove their leadership capabilities. As was noted in Chapter 4, a calm and professional approach is the way to earn respect from fellow team members.

Belbin's work on effective teams

Finding omega managers (see Chapter 2) is not easy. A single person cannot be all things to all people and rarely has all the qualities needed to be excellent in terms of both people and task management. Effective managers, therefore, draw upon the strengths of members of their teams to compensate for weakness they are aware of in themselves. The importance of using the strengths of all team members is summed up neatly in the phrase 'none of us is as smart as all of us'. Dr Belbin's work on team effectiveness is both fascinating and influential, providing useful insights into how *the whole can be greater than the sum of its parts.*

Through his work at the Management College, Henley, Dr Belbin learned to recognize individuals who made a crucial difference to teams. He identified eight clear team-types and to these individuals he gave names. He went on to relate observed team behaviour to psychological traits, using psychometric tests. Dr Belbin and his colleagues then constructed balanced teams containing the eight identified team-types. When set management challenges the balanced teams consistently performed more effectively than teams with random membership. When there were fewer than eight team members then people tended to play more than one role, as necessary.

Belbin's work provides convincing evidence that getting team composition right can be as important as appointing the right individual to be leader. While it is not possible to change the composition of teams in schools easily, a consideration of the team-types that exist in any team may be a very fruitful starting point for analysing the reasons for the under-performance of a particular team. A consideration of Belbin's eight team-types should enable middle managers to recognize themselves and others in their teams. It is important to remember that the names Belbin chose are less important than the characteristics associated with them.

Chairman

Traits:
- stable, dominant, extrovert; s/he may not be the leader of the team so 'chairman' is a misleading term – but s/he certainly has team leadership qualities;
- presides over the team and coordinates its efforts to meet targets;
- intelligent but not brilliant and not an outstandingly creative thinker;
- has self-discipline and integrity;
- has good authority and is often charismatic;

- not domineering but in control in a relaxed way;
- trusts people and is not jealous;
- recognizes the strengths of others and uses them to create a team;
- easy to talk to and a good listener;
- a good communicator;
- capable of making decisions once everyone has had their say.

Shaper

Traits:

- anxious, dominant, extrovert; s/he is likely to be the task leader, even if the chairman is the 'social leader';
- full of nervous energy;
- impulsive and impatient;
- easily frustrated;
- often has rows but does not harbour grudges;
- tries to unite ideas into feasible projects;
- self-confident on the outside but full of self-doubt;
- competitive;
- critical of vague and muddled thinking;
- people often see the shaper as arrogant;
- can make a team feel uncomfortable but does make things happen.

Plant

Traits:

- dominant, high IQ, introvert; Belbin discovered that an ineffective team could be improved by 'planting' one of this type in it;
- full of original ideas and proposals;
- very imaginative in solving problems;
- more concerned with major issues than detail;
- even though introverted s/he is forceful and uninhibited;
- can be prickly and critical of the ideas of others;
- bad at accepting criticism of own ideas.

Monitor evaluator

Traits:

- high IQ, stable, introvert; likely to be serious and not very exciting – main contribution is dispassionate analysis rather than creative ideas – the monitor evaluator will stop the team embarking on misguided projects;

- a constructive critic and clear thinker;
- not highly motivated;
- slow to reach a decision;
- can assimilate and interpret large volumes of complex written material;
- can be tactless when assessing the judgments of others;
- can lower team morale by being a damper;
- dependable but lacks warmth;
- judgment is rarely wrong.

Company worker

Traits:

- stable and controlled, a practical organizer who turns the team's plans into manageable tasks;
- sorts out objectives;
- logical;
- disciplined;
- has integrity;
- doesn't like rapidly changing situations;
- very well organized;
- efficient and systematic;
- can be over-competitive;
- always understands policies and knows what should be being done.

Resource investigator

Traits:

- stable, dominant, extrovert; a very likeable member of the team – relaxed, sociable and enthusiastic;
- tends to drop ideas as quickly as they are taken up;
- gathers information from outside the team;
- makes friends easily;
- diplomatic;
- quick to see the relevance of the ideas of others;
- ineffective without the stimulus of others;
- good under pressure but over-relaxes when it eases.

Team worker

Traits:
- stable, extrovert, low in dominance – very aware of the feelings and needs of team members and senses emotional undercurrents – helps to keep team morale up in a low key way;
- knows about the private lives of team members;
- popular and likeable;
- good communicator and listener;
- loyal and supportive;
- promotes unity;
- dislikes friction and personal confrontation;
- uncompetitive;
- helps team unity;
- works behind the scenes to keep peace.

Finisher

Traits:
- anxious, introvert – the finisher worries about what might go wrong and checks details almost obsessively;
- communicates sense of urgency to others;
- good self-control;
- intolerant towards casual members of the team;
- compulsive about meeting deadlines;
- can lower morale of team by spreading anxiety;
- can miss the bigger picture by concentrating on detail.

In recent years Belbin has modified role titles and identified one extra role (Belbin 1993). These changes are summarized in Table 5.1.

Middle managers in schools could probably recognize the behaviour of members of their teams from the points above and it would probably be beneficial, given the right team ethos, to conduct a fuller assessment of team members as a team development exercise. The important thing is that people identified as being a certain team-type should feel neither inferior nor superior as a result. For success, there is a critical role for each team-type and middle managers should ensure colleagues are used appropriately. If teams are assessed and appear unbalanced in terms of the range of team-types identified then this should be discussed openly. Knowledge is power and although people can't change their personalities they can modify behaviour associated with their personality, if this is necessary to improve team performance. Clearly, any attempt to use Belbin's ideas would need to be handled with great sensitivity and it

Title	Role	Characteristic
Chairperson	Coordinating	Calm, self-confident
Shaper	Team leading	Highly strung, 'driven'
Plant	Innovating	Thinker, innovator, individualistic
Monitor-evaluator	Critical thinking	Sober, unemotional, able to assess, judge and evaluate
Implementer	Getting work done	Practical, common sense, organizing ability
Team worker	Personal relationships	Socially orientated, responds well to people
Completer	Keeping group on its toes	Orderly, painstaking, determined
Resource investigator	Keeping in touch with people outside the organization	Extrovert, wide contacts, likes making links
Specialist	Providing knowledge and skills in rare supply	Single-minded, self-starting, dedicated

Table 5.1   Belbin's team roles

would be unwise for a newly appointed middle manager to look to Belbin as a panacea for problems being encountered with team behaviour. However, an established team, led by a self-critical and respected middle manager, might well be able to use Belbin's ideas as a way of both gaining individual self-knowledge and becoming a more effective team.

What can go wrong with teams?

All kinds of things can go wrong with teams. Team leaders will only improve team ethos and performance by reflecting honestly and critically on the behaviour of their team. A good starting point is to consider your own behaviour – a good team leader usually manages to produce an effective team; a poor team leader usually blames other team members when things are going badly.

- **Meetings**
For many people 'teamwork' and meetings go hand in hand. It is important to realize that meetings can easily wreck, rather than build, teams if they are unnecessary, unproductive and badly managed. Chapter 7 offers advice on how to ensure meetings are effective, but it is worth mentioning at this point that the manager is not automatically the best person to chair every team meeting. It is true that most people assume the manager will chair team meetings because being the chair goes with the role. However, there may be occasions when another member of the team acts as chair, enabling the manager to become one among equals. This is one practical way of encouraging both collegiality and staff development. Whoever chairs a meeting, it is important to ensure that 'action points' are recorded, with named individuals clear about what they have agreed to do and by when.

- **Conflict**
Conflict in teams can occur in situations where there is rivalry between colleagues or fundamental differences of philosophy. Conflict associated with the 'storming' stage of team development is likely to pass, but if conflict is sustained, repetitive and hurtful to individuals it will undermine the team and prevent the growth of a collaborative team culture. This kind of conflict is quite different to the healthy debate and exchange of ideas associated with dynamic teams. Sometimes conflict can result from personality clashes, where two team members dislike one another intensely. This kind of temperamental incompatibility is best dealt with by speaking to each individual separately about the problem to see what ways forward they suggest. Defining their roles clearly can also help, as can praising each one for the particular strengths they bring to the team.

- **Complacency**
In some teams there is little or no debate, little reflection and much defensiveness against criticism or challenge. Such groups have convinced themselves that the team is always right and are only shaken from their complacency by something like a damning OFSTED report. It is most likely that such teams have seen little movement of staff over the years and have not been challenged by senior managers through the appraisal process and target setting. Complacency is a dangerous thing and this is one reason why appointing a new middle manager from outside the school in some circumstances makes more sense than promoting someone from

69

within the team. A new manager joining such a team would need to work hard to change the culture and should not, in the short term, worry too much if team members seem nostalgic about the team they have lost.

Techniques which help teams to develop and succeed

Treating team members decently, as outlined in Chapter 4, is important for getting the most out of individuals. However, as we have seen in this chapter, a team is more than the sum of its parts and there are certain practical devices which can assist in getting group members working as a team.

- **Brainstorming**
  Most teachers are aware of brainstorming – the generation of as many ideas as quickly as possible by a group of people – and many teachers use the technique effectively in their teaching. Brainstorming can be a useful team-building tool because it can be fun, it encourages contributions from all team members and it creates the kind of 'clean communication' which helps teams to become dynamic and creative. When a brainstorm goes well it builds confidence and gives a team a real sense of achievement. Brainstorming sessions are especially useful for helping to integrate newly appointed colleagues into a team. If brainstorms are to be successful it is important to remember that every idea is recorded; no idea is evaluated at the brainstorm stage and the team leader does not have to be the scribe.

- **The PEP talk**
  PEP stands for 'Planning Effective Performance'. It consists of three simple questions: What did we do that worked well? What did we do that didn't work well? What shall we do next time? PEP talks should focus on moving forward and should avoid recriminations. PEP talks can be long or short depending on the event or issue under review. They can be used to evaluate almost any team activity: field trips, public events and new courses are just three examples. Of course, it is vital that, having engaged a team in the PEP talk process, conclusions reached are acted upon. If they are not then people will simply become cynical and put no real effort into the process when it is used again.

- **Development plans and action plans**

  Development planning is now well established in schools and the cycle of audit–plan–implement–review is used with varying degrees of success. A more detailed exploration of managing development is provided in Chapter 9; the important point to make at this stage is that development planning must be a collective activity. Sharing views about what has been achieved and deciding together on objectives, individual responsibilities and success criteria is crucial to team effectiveness. It is also vital if teachers are to feel both empowerment and accountability.

Self-assessment and reflection

As a middle manager it is important to reflect on your capacity for creating an effective team. I have included a number of scaled questions below which should help you identify your strengths and weaknesses. These questions are based loosely on a series of questions by Maddux (1986) and modified to suit a school context. Circle the number that best reflects where you fall on the scale. The higher the number, the more the characteristic describes you. When you have finished total the numbers circled and look at the comment that goes with your score. Don't despair if your attitudes have generated negative comments. The important thing is to plan to modify your behaviour so that you are doing all you can to create an effective team.

If I could appoint a new member of my team I would select someone with good inter-personal skills ahead of someone with excellent academic qualifications.

7 6 5 4 3 2 1

I help my team develop a sense of ownership by involving them in problem solving, policy writing and goal setting.

7 6 5 4 3 2 1

I try to provide team spirit by encouraging colleagues to work with new team members on certain tasks.

7 6 5 4 3 2 1

I talk to people openly and honestly and encourage the same kind of communication in return.

7 6 5 4 3 2 1

I always try and keep my word. If I have promised a colleague something I always deliver because their trust is important to me.	7 6 5 4 3 2 1
I use activities such as brainstorms with my team as a means of generating trust and respect between team members.	7 6 5 4 3 2 1
I try and use directing, coaching, supporting and delegating as appropriate to individual team members.	7 6 5 4 3 2 1
I understand that conflict within groups is normal, but work to resolve it quickly and fairly before it can become destructive.	7 6 5 4 3 2 1
I believe people perform as a team when they know what is expected and what the benefits are.	7 6 5 4 3 2 1
I am not frightened of tackling team members who under-perform.	7 6 5 4 3 2 1

What your score indicates

- A score between 60 and 70 indicates a positive attitude towards colleagues and the type of attitude needed to build and maintain a strong team. You appear to be an empowering leader, capable of raising and maintaining morale.
- A score between 40 and 59 is acceptable and with reasonable effort you should be able to lead an effective team. Even so, you should think carefully about your approach. Are there ways in which you can be even more positive with members of your team?
- A score below 40 means you need to examine your behaviour towards colleagues and reflect critically on your management philosophy. Do you praise enough? Do you empower? Do you act with integrity? Do you recognize the need to team build? Are you publicly enthusiastic?

Summary

A team is more than a group of people placed together because they have some aspect of their work in common. A team is characterized by:

- members sharing a vision;
- members being interdependent;
- members knowing what the team's goals are;
- members understanding what their unique contribution to achieving the goals is;
- members communicating openly;
- members supporting and trusting one another;
- healthy debate between members;
- relaxed but purposeful relationships.

A successful team is creative and flexible and the achievements of the team are greater than the achievements of individuals in the team working separately would be. A successful team is likely to be led by a manager who encourages collaboration and empowerment, who trusts and praises individuals in the team and who is receptive to new ideas and opportunities.

The greatest threats to team effectiveness are unproductive meetings, rivalry between team members, personality clashes and complacency. Middle managers can encourage teamwork through the use of collaborative communication devices such as brainstorms, PEPs and collective development planning.

CHAPTER SIX

Effective Communication

Introduction

Communication is an activity which takes place when a message is transferred satisfactorily from one party to another. For communication to take place there has to be a source, transmission through channels and a receiver. Middle managers have to communicate with a wide range of client groups and need to make their chosen style and language (spoken or written) *fit for purpose*. The Teacher Training Agency spells out the need for effective communication by stating that subject leaders should have 'the ability to make points clearly and understand the views of others' (TTA 1998). This phrase is useful as it reminds us that communication should be a two-way exchange; negotiation in communication is often vital if the message is to be fully received, accepted by the parties concerned and acted upon.

Poor communication lies at the heart of many misunderstandings and disputes that arise in secondary schools. Even in teams that have cultivated a positive ethos and where collaboration is well established, team leaders often have to make decisions 'on the hoof' and failure to inform colleagues of these can cause resentment. Of course, occasional failures of communication will be tolerated if the foundation stones of good management are in place, but when poor communication becomes habitual it can undermine good team relationships. In other teams it can be the failure to communicate clearly and effectively which is the barrier to creating a sharing and supportive team culture. In teams where there are comments like 'I always seem to be the last person to find out what's going on in this school' and 'what exactly are we doing before the next team meeting then?' there is clearly cause for concern.

One problem is that communication skills are frequently taken for granted. It is assumed that colleagues who speak the same language need only the time, effort and sincerity to communicate successfully. As communication is a fundamental teaching tool newly appointed managers often feel that they don't need to develop this skill. This is not usually the case and managers need to analyse and reflect on their communication skills as on all other aspects of management. Just as teachers refine their classroom style over the years so team leaders learn how to communicate with greater proficiency as they become more experienced. If you are a prospective or newly appointed middle managers this chapter should help you to avoid making basic mistakes with communication and thus help you to establish yourself more smoothly in a management role.

Middle managers and communication networks

Middle managers operate extensive communication networks. A typical communication network for a head of department is shown in Table 6.1. It will be slightly different for other middle managers.

As a head of department you do not have to communicate actively with all the groups all the time, but you should be aware of the range of 'client groups' you may have to make contact with. Generally speaking communication will be more formal with people in the 'Occasional' category than with people in the 'Daily' category. However, there may be exceptions to this rule: regular contact with colleagues in other schools may result in a very healthy and relaxed approach to communication, for example. Also, much will depend on the personalities of the particular

Daily communication	*Regular* communication	*Occasional* communication
Members of department Pupils in your classes (Students on ITT)	Head of faculty Other heads of department Senior management Governors Pastoral heads Support staff Pupils beyond your own classes Parents	HE and FE establishments Other schools Local community Local industry Exam boards HMI OFSTED LEA advisors The media Past pupils

Formality of communication increases →

Table 6.1   Communication network of a middle manager

people in each group. There may be some people who change categories over time. For example, students on ITT may need to be seen every day in the early stages of their training but less regularly as their skill levels develop.

Networking, the activity of developing personal contacts, is endemic to organizations. It is quite useful for middle managers in secondary schools to share information, ideas and concerns with colleagues in similar management roles from their own school and other schools. Being aware of what other year heads think about a particular policy proposal that will impact on your role as year head is perfectly legitimate, for example. Middle managers need to be aware though that by identifying with a particular group there may be negative side effects, especially in schools which have not developed a shared sense of purpose and collaborative ways of working.

Making communication effective

Effective communication is more likely to occur in collaborative team or school cultures, where people are valued, encouraged to voice their opinions and supported than in hierarchical institutions. When people feel trusted, secure and confident they are much more likely to admit to not understanding messages given or to engage in debate as a means of achieving agreed meanings. In more rigid teams and schools a climate of closed communication is likely to exist, with greater competition between team members and control maintained in part through suppression of information. Two contrasting communication climates are outlined in Table 6.2.

There are various communication flows which exist within institutions and teams (Lewis 1975). Two contrasting arrangements are the chain and the all-channel model illustrated in Figure 6.1. The chain is associated with hierarchical cultures with a line-management approach. Communication tends to be instructional which can work with simple tasks, but morale tends to be low at the end of the chain. The all-channel model seems most effective for complex tasks and would be the favoured approach of managers wanting to generate a collaborative culture in which the views of professionals are encouraged and valued.

Encouraging an open communication climate in your team is important and the team meeting is the obvious place for the all-channel model to be encouraged.

Effective communication involves making appropriate use of a variety of communication techniques: formal, informal, oral and written – *fitness for purpose* is the important thing. It is essential that the people you

77

Open communication climate	Closed communication climate
Communication encourages and values everyone, regardless of status	Communication emphasizes differences in status
Communication shows empathy and understanding	Communication is impersonal
Feedback and debate are encouraged	Little discussion is allowed
There is a focus on collective problem-solving	Decisions are made by a few who hold positions of power
Statements are informative not evaluative	Statements are judgemental
Error is recognized and minimized	People are blamed
There are no hidden messages	Messages hold hidden meaning

Table 6.2   Communication climates

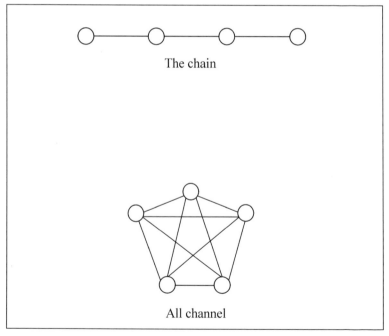

Figure 6.1   Contrasting communication flows

communicate with feel that your choice of method is appropriate; this means being sensitive to people's needs. Two examples will illustrate this point.

- **Example 1**
  A head of department needs to tell a member of her team that she has had to change his next year's timetable in a way that might not please him. She does this in a memo. The information is communicated, but not in the right way. In this instance the head of department should have given the team member an explanation which would have been best achieved in a face-to-face conversation.

- **Example 2**
  A year tutor receives a note from a parent, about an incident the parent would like to discuss. The year tutor sends a quick handwritten note back saying that he will be in touch soon. This is an inappropriate response which will reflect badly on the school. The parent deserved a telephone call or a more formal reply, properly typed. It is not unreasonable for the year tutor to delay a meeting, but the method used to communicate this was unprofessional.

Verbal communication skills

Most communication is verbal and it is theoretically a very efficient form of communication which allows the transmission of complex information from one person to another. Thoughtful and reflective managers can get the basics of this form of communication right by thinking about their listening and speaking, their social skills and how best to create understanding.

Listening and speaking

Listening requires an awareness of bias, visual signals and vocal sounds.
- **Bias**
  Everyone's point of view includes bias of some kind. Being aware of this should help to prevent managers from dismissing the views of others too readily. It is important not to make assumptions about the likely views of colleagues and so pre-judge their ideas or arguments. By being open minded and encouraging a range of ideas team leaders help to generate trust, real debate and collaboration from their team.

- **Visual signals**
  A visual sign is body language. People interpret the meaning of body

language according to their own understanding, usually based on background, upbringing and experience. Even so, appropriate gestures can add considerable meaning to communication. Listening is obviously enhanced when eye contact is made with the speaker and people will be encouraged to contribute when they can see they have the full attention of the listener. A body turned away from a speaker is very discouraging, for example.

- **Vocal sounds**
  Listening to the sound and tone of a speaker's voice enhances understanding. Sometimes there are hidden meanings which can be read from the tone being used. Speakers signal an emotional state through their voice more than their choice of words and it is important for a manager to tune in to the message being conveyed.

Speaking effectively requires tuning in to the listener's needs and pacing what is said accordingly. It is important for managers to speak to people not at them. This means giving people the opportunity to respond to statements made so that a dialogue can take place. Speakers communicate warmth, interest and authority through their voice and those who vary their tone and rhythm are usually more engaging and interesting than those who don't. Humour in tone and content is a good way to relax people and need not detract from serious points you are trying to make.

Social skills

Socially skilled information exchange occurs when the leader:
- has clear goals to be achieved through the communication;
- behaves in a way that conveys a consistent overall impression; eye contact, facial expression, tone of voice and body language support the message being given in words;
- chooses an appropriate time and situation to convey the message.

Creating understanding

It is the leader's responsibility to open a debate, encourage colleagues' contributions and guide discussion so that a common understanding emerges within the group. This enhances a group's sense of purpose and clarifies the team vision.

Newly appointed managers can feel very threatened when difficult issues are discussed and team members present their opinions forcefully, especially if there appears to be opposition to the views presented by the manager. Leaders committed to encouraging a collaborative culture turn such discussions to their advantage by attentive listening and setting a tone of tolerant discussion. Respect generates respect and it is a manager's duty to set the right tone. The key task is to achieve a balance between creative exchange of views and a free-for-all, where the loudest voice gets heard most. Managing meetings is covered in more detail in Chapter 7 but at this point it is worth mentioning three important skills which managers should develop in order to facilitate effective group discussions.

- First, managers must insist that people speak one at a time through the chair. This prevents the loudest and most confident team members dominating discussions and encourages the participation of everybody.
- Secondly, the leader must learn to keep a discussion on track. If there is too much digression from the main point then the leader should paraphrase what has just been said, making links to the key issue under discussion. This should be done in a non-judgemental manner so as not to discourage the colleague responsible for the digression. A good example of when to use this technique is when teachers introduce long anecdotes about particular pupils they have taught to illustrate discussion points.
- Thirdly, team leaders need to be willing to intervene if two or more colleagues become locked in a dispute. The leader's task is to take attention away from the disputing participants and focus on the issues which they raised. Encouraging the rest of the group to discuss the controversial issue in order to find a solution best does this. Changing the subject is not a good strategy as it leaves the issue unresolved and likely to flare up again at some point in the future.

Barriers to effective verbal communication

Communication is ineffective when the receiver ends up with a different understanding to that intended by the transmitter of the message. This can be caused by poor communication skills on the part of the sender but barriers to effective communication also arise as a result of a climate of mistrust. For example, if managers make a habit of saying one thing but doing another it should not be surprising if their messages cease to be accepted at face value.

The most common barriers to communication are:

- **Semantics** – different words have different meanings and words can be interpreted differently by different people. It is very important, therefore, that everybody uses the same definitions. In teams and departments this means discussing what words mean, especially important when issues such as racist behaviour and harassment are being debated. Parents sometimes need words used regularly by teachers explaining – the difference between a test and an exam, for example.

- **Status** – in schools and departments that are hierarchical status can become a barrier to effective communication. Junior colleagues can feel reluctant to ask for clarification if a communication is unclear because they fear looking stupid in the eyes of older and more senior colleagues. This is one reason why it is so important to build an ethos of trust and support in a team which means no one is ever embarrassed to admit they don't understand something.

- **Cultural and gender differences** – if managers are insensitive to differences of interpretation of words and non-verbal signals that can result from gender or cultural differences they will not be effective communicators. Putting people at their ease is necessary if a relaxed team ethos is to be built; this means team members being sensitive to the feelings and expectations of others. Physical contact is an example of behaviour which can produce very positive or very negative responses depending on the interpretation attached to it. The manager must set the tone by getting to know each team member individually and by showing appropriate respect and sensitivity.

- **Information overload** – when the timing and content of a communication is inappropriate people may fail to act on it. Even very loyal and hardworking colleagues reach saturation point and are simply unable to take more information on board. Too many items on the agenda of a team meeting can result in information overload, for example.

The importance of being assertive

Much has been made in this book so far of the need to encourage collaboration and openness in your team and in this chapter open communication has been advocated. In teams where members trust and support one another people are encouraged to be assertive. Being assertive means taking responsibility for our behaviour, having respect for ourselves and others and being honest. It allows us to say what we want or feel but not at other people's expense. It means understanding the point of view of other people and being self-confident and positive. It is not about winning come what may or getting our own way all of the time. Assertiveness is about handling conflict and coming to an acceptable compromise.

At some stage middle managers are sure to encounter people who are aggressive and people who are passive. Being aggressive means getting your own way at the expense of others and making them feel worthless or incompetent. Being passive means ignoring your interests and allowing others to manipulate you by denying how you really think or feel. It is important that middle managers are neither aggressive nor passive and that they encourage assertiveness in other team members. Not only is this morally right but it creates a stronger, more dynamic and more able team and ensures that honest communication occurs. Middle managers should learn to recognize passive, assertive and aggressive behaviour in order to be able to respond appropriately (see Table 6.3).

It is especially important to recognize signs of aggression when dealing with angry parents. Responding inappropriately to these signs could be potentially very dangerous. How we listen, how we respond and our body language can help us to diffuse conflict situations. Whenever a parent, colleague or pupil has what they regard as a grievance it is important to listen, show understanding and ask questions. If you feel their anger is misguided it is tempting to state your position firmly but it would be wrong to do this when they are full of anger. By listening and showing empathy a dangerous situation can be diffused; there will be opportunities to explain your position later. By avoiding aggressive body language yourself you help to calm the anger in others.

This does not, of course, mean you have to 'give in' to unreasonable people. Your aim will be to come to a joint agreement on action and this is more likely to be achieved by allowing a person who is 'worked up' to have their say first. Once an angry person has calmed down and you have convinced them of your concern and sincerity things can begin to move forward. It is important that any grievance is fully investigated and, once the facts are known, your position can be stated firmly and an appropriate way forward negotiated with the parent (or colleague or pupil) concerned. The important thing is that by using appropriate communication skills in a heated situation you have prevented an escalation of anger into violence. Remember, listening shows cooperation, showing understanding indicates you care and asking questions allows you to gain control. Good teachers use these techniques with pupils and effective managers use them also.

	Passive	*Assertive*	*Aggressive*
Verbal content	• Rambling • Apologies • Self put-downs • Frequent justifications	• Clear statements • Distinctions between fact and opinion • Questions to find out opinions of others • Ways of resolving problems	• Boastfulness • Opinions expressed as fact • Threats • Blame put on others • Sarcasm
Voice and speech	• Wobbly • Soft • Monotone • Pauses • Frequent throat clearing	• Steady • Rich and warm • Clear • Fluent • Emphasizes key words	• Very firm • Cold • Strident • Loud • Abrupt • Emphasizes blaming words
Face and eyes	• Evasive • Looking down	• Smiles when pleased • Frowns when angry • Firm eye contact	• Scowls • Eyebrows raised in amazement • Tries to stare-down
Body language	• Arms crossed (protection) • Hand-wringing • Shrugs • Mouth covered	• Open hand movements • Sits upright but relaxed • Stands with head held up	• Finger pointing • Fist thumping • Sits upright • Stands tall • Strides around • Arms crossed

Table 6.3   Passive, assertive and aggressive behaviour

Written communication

Middle managers in schools need to be able to communicate clearly in writing. They are accountable to a range of different client groups and need to think carefully about the needs and expectations of the audience they are communicating with. As with many other areas of management *fitness for purpose* is the important consideration: a memo to a colleague will clearly be written in a very different style to a report for governors, for example.

Middle managers are usually involved with communicating in writing with the various groups listed in Table 6.1. The range of documents they will have to prepare will include: worksheets and booklets for pupils; memos and minutes for colleagues; reports for senior staff and governors; progress reports for pupils and parents; a departmental or team handbook; schemes of work; mark schemes; development plans; materials promoting courses; press releases; and a range of letters to various people.

The tools of written communication are sound grammar, accurate spelling, structure and punctuation. In formal documents each sentence needs to be effective and it makes sense to use the following steps: pre-writing; drafting; revising; editing; printing. Good word processing skills are essential as the use of a computer is bound to save you time, even if you have some degree of secretarial support for producing documents.

- **Pre-writing**
  This stage involves the gathering of ideas, for example by brainstorming a series of developments chronologically or listing the advantages and disadvantages of a particular proposal.

- **Drafting**
  This stage involves the initial production of the document. You need to focus and structure the ideas you generated in pre-writing into an order and format that will make sense for your chosen audience.

- **Revising**
  Revising involves reading your document carefully to determine whether it delivers its intended message for its intended audience. At this stage you may add new material, delete inappropriate material and rearrange the order of information to achieve maximum effect.

- **Editing**
  You now need to check spelling, grammar, punctuation and tone to ensure that the finished document is accurate and polished.

- **Printing**
  Ensure that the finished product looks good by using a laser printer or good inkjet printer. Ensure that pages are numbered and that the front cover does justice to the contents. It is a good idea for subject departments to develop a 'house-style' in order to market themselves both internally and externally (see next section).

Communication and marketing

Many teachers still feel that marketing has little to do with teaching. They associate marketing with the commercial world and with persuading people, often by exaggerated claims, to part with their money. Marketing, they feel, is *gloss at the expense of substance*. If schools see marketing simply as *promotion* then there is a real danger that their marketing will simply become an 'add on' and that their glossy brochures will bear little resemblance to the reality of everyday school life. However, schools are increasingly competing for pupils and it is important that they communicate their strengths and achievements effectively. Likewise, departments in secondary schools are to an extent competing for pupils at Key Stage 4 and Key Stage 5 when subject choices are made. It is sensible, therefore, for a department to generate a positive image.

Many schools and departments go further with marketing, though, seeing it as an integral part of the management process and using marketing to help with quality assurance. Marketing in such schools is characterized by the following attitudes:

- **Marketing is more than promotion**

  Marketing is seen as a process not an event. The clients (mainly students and parents) are involved in the process. They are asked their views about the quality of services provided through market research and their opinions are taken into account when planning for improvement. In such schools it is quite normal for pupils to be consulted through questionnaires and interviews about courses, preferred teaching and learning styles and pastoral support. The schools try to focus on the services they provide through the eyes of the users rather than simply as providers, in an effort to improve quality and satisfaction. Marketing is not an 'add on' it is part of the continuous process of school improvement.

- **Marketing is internal as well as external**

  Marketing is traditionally associated with conveying the right image to those outside the organization. In the case of schools this means prospective pupils and parents, the local community, prospective staff, the LEA, OFSTED, FE/HE and so on. Schools taking marketing seriously realize that communicating effectively with internal clients is equally important. This doesn't just mean existing parents but includes current staff, pupils, governors and any regular visitors or helpers. Promoting the achievements of the school or 'talking up' the department is done continually and helps to maintain a positive ethos and a feeling of success.

In order to communicate an effective image the staff (teaching and others) and governors must have a 'corporate perspective'. This means being clear about the mission and goals of the school (and department/team). This is why some schools spend much time on developing a coherent view of the school, agreeing its aims and values and making sure these are reflected in development plans before producing marketing materials. There is little point trying to promote a product which is ill defined or the suppliers have no faith in; this is why it is vital to create a shared school vision as the foundation for school development and marketing. It is worth noting that Sammons *et al.* (1995) found shared vision and goals to be a key characteristic of effective schools in the work they undertook for OFSTED.

- **Marketing is everyone's job**
  Even though a senior member of staff may be the marketing coordinator it is important that everyone working in a school sees marketing as their job. The way a receptionist deals with parents or the manner in which a teacher handles a complaint from a student are aspects of marketing. Indeed, a single incident badly handled can undo much that has been achieved in creating a positive image of a school. At departmental level it is easy to see that an ineffective teacher of Year 9 classes will have much more impact on pupils' likelihood of choosing the subject for GCSE than publicity leaflets created by the department. If departments are providing good standards of teaching and treating their students with the respect they deserve then marketing their courses should be relatively easy.

Reflection on marketing

To an extent middle managers will be influenced in marketing by the school marketing policy. For example, in some schools heads of department are free to make contacts with the local media whereas in others they must go through the marketing coordinator. Whatever policy is in operation the following questions are worth asking. They are not in any order of priority and the list is not an exhaustive one. Nevertheless, they should raise awareness of the numerous ways in which an image of themselves and their team is being created and ways in which their work could be more 'client focused'.

- Does the way I deal with colleagues beyond my immediate team reflect well on my area and me?

- Do my memos create a professional image for my area? Do we have a 'house style'?
- Do I take enough care with the appearance and content of documents I produce for people?
- Do the display boards in my area create a good impression of the work of my team?
- Does my area have a corporate identity?
- Do we produce accessible and interesting course guides for students, especially when they are choosing between courses?
- Do we use flyers, posters and newsletters to promote the work and achievements of our area?
- Do we involve students in evaluating courses?
- Do we use students to promote our area to other students and parents?
- Do we make use of the local media in promoting the newsworthy things we are engaged in?
- Do I keep senior colleagues informed about all the good things colleagues in my area are engaged in?
- Do I use team meetings and staff briefings as opportunities to celebrate achievements and praise the work of colleagues in my team?
- Do we praise students enough and do we publicize achievements of pupils in our area more widely, for example through assemblies?
- Are we welcoming to visitors?
- Do we create a good impression on parents' evenings?
- Are letters and reports to parents of a high enough standard?
- Do we listen to our students?
- Are we accessible to students?
- Do I take student complaints seriously?

It may be that you are the leader of a team providing a very good education to your students but simply not sharing your achievements with others. It is just as important not to be shy about announcing the achievements of your team as it is not to exaggerate their successes and make false claims. Informing others of the successes of staff and pupils in your area is important for several reasons:

- As a middle manager you should be keeping senior managers informed of developments in your area. They need to know what colleagues are doing so that when they evaluate their performance or write references a clear picture exists.
- The public praising of colleagues for their successes raises self-esteem and increases motivation.
- The public praising of students for their successes raises self-esteem and increases motivation.

- The public sharing of achievements in one area of school can encourage other areas of school to reflect on their own achievements.
- It is important that all pupils and parents know about the successes of their school even if they are not directly involved. This increases confidence in the institution and is good marketing.

Reflection on departmental documents

Over the past two decades schools have been made increasingly accountable and middle managers need to ensure that they can provide a range of stake-holders with information they might require. In most schools there will be agreements about what information needs to be held at team level and which needs to be lodged with senior managers. If you are a head of department could you answer 'yes' to the following questions?

- If a new pupil arrived from abroad would you be able to provide her parents with written information about your department and about the syllabus she would be following? Would you be able to provide a scheme of work that would help the pupil and her parents to understand how you were applying the national curriculum or GCSE syllabus and see clearly what work had been missed?
- If a local education authority inspector arrived in school and wanted to see information about your department would you be able to provide it? Is your handbook up to date? Do you have a staffing structure/responsibilities diagram in it? Are there copies of your team's current timetables available? Is your departmental development plan up to date, including an indication of progress made with targets since they were set? Are you able to demonstrate value-added in your subject?
- If a parent wanted to know how her son was doing in your subject would you be able to show her? Does a portfolio of his work relating to the national curriculum or GCSE course exist? Are you able to show how he is doing compared with national expectations for pupils of his age? Are you able to show how he is doing compared with other pupils in your school? Are you able to demonstrate progress being made over time, especially between end of key stage assessments?

Documents relating to all of the above ought to exist. If they don't, then planning for their introduction ought to become part of your development plan. It is likely that assessment is handled as a whole-school issue and that models for demonstrating value-added or comparing departmental performance are organized by a senior member of staff. Even so, the data generated ought to be with your department, as your team needs to be considering it in planning for future improvements in performance.

It is not necessary to go over the top with documents. Some heads of department can show beautifully produced, detailed documents which are more gloss than substance and do not reflect what is really happening in their subject. Quality in the classroom from all team members is a head of department's primary aim. Clear planning, agreed schemes of work and systematic assessment procedures are important foundations of quality in the classroom. Documents for internal use relating to these areas must be in place. However, departments must also have a range of documents to meet the needs of clients. A concise handbook, a leaflet or flyer promoting the work of the department and a 'pupil-speak' version of syllabi and assessment criteria are essential. It does not have to be the head of department who produces all these, of course. Tasks relating to documents can be agreed when the development plan is being written. Once in place, documents should be reviewed and updated annually.

Summary

Communication is central to the operation of an effective school and it is important that middle managers are skilled in communication techniques. An open and supportive team culture in which colleagues feel valued and secure is likely to promote open communication between members. Team leaders need to encourage new members to be honest and open by being clear and supportive in their own style of communication and by providing opportunities for newcomers to contribute and express their views.

Middle managers are involved in communicating with a wide range of people and must be able to adapt their style accordingly. Effective communication involves a range of strategies from informal discussions to formal written reports. Skilled communicators consider *fitness for purpose* when deciding which communication technique to employ. By seeing all people being communicated with as 'clients' (internal and external) team leaders begin to think about the need for clarity and quality in their communications. Considering what it would be like to be on the receiving end of your own communications is something middle managers need to do, however busy they may be.

Verbal and non-verbal communication involves listening and observing. Being an effective listener is very important and encourages others to be open in their communication. As a middle manager you need to be assertive but not aggressive and you should encourage and develop assertiveness in your team members. If people feel both relaxed enough and confident enough to speak their minds a more dynamic team with shared and understood goals is likely to develop. This is far better than a passive team with no dynamism or a team that accepts what you say to your face but then moans and undermines your ideas behind your back.

As schools become increasingly self-sufficient and concerned about maintaining or improving their market position creating a positive image becomes a high priority. Middle managers have their part to play in this and should ensure that their communications reflect well on their teams and the school. By publicizing the achievements of their team and their pupils middle managers are helping to market their area and the school and to contribute to raising morale. As well as producing quality material for school brochures, flyers, newsletters and the media, middle managers need to be mindful that every interaction they engage in with colleagues, pupils, parents and others is an act of marketing. Pupils going home disgruntled and complaining to their parents because an incident has been handled badly can produce negative publicity which easily undermines the positive image being conveyed through the school's published materials.

CHAPTER SEVEN

Meetings

Introduction

Meetings are essential to the effective operation of a team. Sadly, far too many take place that are unproductive or even dysfunctional. Newly appointed middle managers are all too aware that over the years they have attended many meetings which they regarded as a waste of time and which they were resentful of, given all the other things they could have done with the time. Organizing successful meetings can be a demanding aspect of middle management and one that is sometimes a source of considerable stress to the inexperienced.

However, *effective* meetings have several advantages: they allow for clear communication; they improve staff skills in decision-making; they provide a sense of involvement among team members; they improve job satisfaction; they increase commitment; and they ensure that managers and their team are 'speaking the same language'. The essential thing is to make meetings productive. This chapter considers the factors and conditions that create successful meetings and provides some straightforward and pragmatic guidelines for ensuring your meetings are successful.

Why meet at all?

The number of meetings held in a school will reflect the size and culture of the school. In most schools a schedule of meetings is drawn up before the academic year commences to ensure that all teams (academic, pastoral, key-stage etc.) are provided with fair and adequate meeting time within the 1265 hours of teachers' contracted time. This usually means having a rota of regular meetings. The advantage of this approach is that teams have regular scheduled meetings; the disadvantage is that there are some times in the year when meetings are not really needed and other times when additional meetings are needed because a team's workload is not evenly distributed throughout the year. For example, subject teams often require additional meetings when moderating GCSE course work. Ideally, there should be a schedule of meetings, with team leaders empowered to decide whether or not it is necessary to meet rather than feeling obliged to meet because of 1265 hours.

In a team and a school with a collegiate approach to work, where colleagues feel valued and trusted, there is likely to be flexibility over meetings, with meetings that are additions to those identified on the schedule being called *if necessary*. The important phrase here is *if necessary*. When colleagues can see the need for a meeting and when the meeting is conducted in a way that produces clear outcomes there will be little resentment about attending. However, when people are forced to attend irrelevant and unproductive meetings simply because they are on a schedule, a '1265 mentality' can result in which teachers are unwilling to attend meetings not on the schedule. This mentality is associated with the Newtonian culture described in Chapter 2 and needs to be avoided at all costs.

If you decide to hold a meeting do all members of your team need to attend? If you are considering major issues or are brainstorming new ideas on policy and philosophy the answer is clearly 'yes'. However, there is little point in colleagues attending a meeting about the A-level syllabus if they are not and will not be involved in teaching it, for example. Thinking about the order of your agenda can help. By having information-giving and whole-team issues first all colleagues in the team can be involved, but then only those people connected with the agenda items which follow need remain. However, do bear in mind the points made about agenda writing given below.

Different types of meeting

If meetings are to be effective then all staff need to understand their function. Middle managers are required to plan, lead and participate in meetings which may have one or more of the following functions:
- to inform;
- to decide;
- to generate ideas;
- to problem-solve;
- to consult;
- to negotiate;
- to plan;
- to allocate;
- to motivate.

It is very important to be clear about the purpose(s) of a meeting and the balance within it. For example, it would be inappropriate to use a 60-minute meeting simply for information giving. Likewise, in a meeting devoted to generating ideas (strategic discussion) it would be unproductive to get bogged down in the minutiae of how a new policy might work in detail (operational discussion). Strategic discussions would be best kept to one meeting with operational considerations for another. In this way more will be achieved.

Steps to effective meetings

Before the meeting

1. Plan the meeting carefully by asking the following questions:
   - Who should attend?
   - What is the purpose of the meeting?
   - Where and when will it be held?
   - How many items will be on the agenda?
   - What briefing papers are needed?
2. Prepare and send out the agenda and briefing papers well in advance of the meeting (a week is usually fine). Think carefully about the agenda. You might want routine business first because you only need certain colleagues to stay on and discuss later items which directly concern them. It is equally possible that you have a major issue to discuss that concerns everyone. Should this be the first item on the agenda? If it isn't then there is a danger that routine matters and announcements will use up valuable time needed for discussing the major issue, unless the meeting is very tightly chaired. Ensure that there are not too many items on any one agenda; between three and five is usually a manageable number for a meeting of an hour. As team leader it is vital that you have prepared yourself for each item on the agenda so that you can provide clear thinking and answer any questions posed by the team.
3. Try to hold the meeting in a pleasant room and get there early to arrange the chairs. Different types of meeting work best with different seating arrangements (see below) and so you must ensure that the seating is *fit for purpose*. Providing refreshments is always appreciated by colleagues and helps to set a relaxed tone, as well as preventing late arrivals using the excuse that they were desperate for a drink and had to wait for the kettle to boil! Don't time your after-school meetings to start immediately the school bell goes. Give people ten minutes to gather their thoughts. A 50-minute meeting

which begins promptly at 3.40 is likely to be more productive than a 60-minute meeting that is supposed to start at 3.30 but never does. A sloppy start to a meeting sets the wrong tone.

At the beginning of the meeting

1. Always start on time; this sets an appropriate businesslike tone and means you are more likely to finish on time. Remember, there is no conflict between having a relaxed and collegiate team ethos and being businesslike in meetings. People appreciate meetings that are run properly.

2. Clearly define roles within the meeting. Who is acting as chair, who is taking minutes and is anyone providing a specialist input? Although it is assumed that the team leader will be chair this doesn't have to be the case for every meeting. A team leader may wish to give a colleague the experience of running a meeting as part of their development, for example. If the meeting is a decision-making meeting where a vote is being taken the team leader might think it fairer to allow a colleague to chair so that they can express a view from the floor, with no danger of showing bias in the way they handle the discussion. It is a good idea to rotate minute writing as this spreads the work load, gives experience to newcomers and prevents the chair of the meeting giving a particular 'flavour' to the decisions made. On a practical note it is actually quite difficult for one person to chair a meeting effectively and make notes, however brief.

3. Review, revise and order the agenda. It may be that since the agenda was issued something urgent has occurred which needs addressing in preference to some routine items on the agenda, or a colleague who was due to contribute an item to the meeting may be ill, for example.

4. Remind colleagues of the time at which the meeting will end and, if necessary, remind them that there are time limits on certain agenda items. This helps to focus people's minds and, with effective chairing, prevents the meeting wandering off track.

5. Always review the action points from the previous meeting. If people are used to meetings being closed with clear action points and opened with a review of these it is more likely that they will be efficient in completing the action agreed. It also means that if action points have not been achieved some thought can be given to how best to move things forward. Being accountable to the team is an important aspect of the collegiate culture and being supported towards achieving goals is more likely if these goals are regularly reviewed.

6. If there are guests at your meeting or if you are chairing a meeting for the first time it is polite to ask all participants to introduce themselves. If you are chairing a one-off meeting it is important to ask all participants what they hope to get out of the meeting.

During the meeting

During the meeting the chairperson must adopt a style *fit for purpose* (see below), but whatever the nature of the meeting it is important to:
- keep to time;
- keep people on task;
- ensure action points are clear.

At the end of the meeting

1. Remind people of action points agreed upon during the meeting: who, what, when?
2. Set the date and time of the next meeting and develop a preliminary agenda. It might be that some non-essential items from the current meeting have been deferred or that a team member is going on a course and needs an opportunity to report back at the next meeting.
3. Evaluate the meeting. This does not mean asking everyone to complete a questionnaire! It simply means giving people the chance to say whether or not they feel the aims of the meeting have been met. If people feel disgruntled that an issue has not been adequately debated it is better that they say so rather than leaving the meeting unhappy and uncommitted to a decision made.
4. Close the meeting crisply and positively. Generally, it is important to finish on time or even a few minutes early. However, on occasions members may decide to prolong a meeting by an agreed amount so as to get business finished or to prevent the need for another meeting. There is a big difference between meetings regularly over-running due to being badly chaired and an occasional meeting being extended due to unforeseen difficulties with a particular item. Remember, though, that for some colleagues extending a meeting may be very inconvenient as they might have other commitments to meet. It is not fair to exclude people from participation simply because they cannot alter their domestic arrangements at the drop of a hat.
5. Clean up the room and rearrange the furniture.

After the meeting

1. Liaise with the minute taker, if appropriate, to ensure that the minutes are accurate and efficiently written up and distributed. With most colleagues you will simply need to thank them for taking the minutes but do nothing else, whereas with a new team member they may feel happier if you have seen the minutes before they are distributed to other colleagues. Keep the minutes brief by reducing each item on the agenda to outcomes: the agreed action points – who, when and where? In some schools a standardized pro-forma for minutes exists and administrative staff type minutes of meetings up. This is an excellent idea for two reasons. First, a regular moan from teachers is that they do too much administration – here is one simple way senior managers can be supportive in reducing administration. Secondly, minutes in a standardized form are easier for senior colleagues to digest and need only contain essential information, namely the agreed action points but not unnecessary detail about who said what. In schools where no such arrangements exist middle managers would be advised to act together to explain the benefits of such a system to senior staff.

2. Monitor action points, as necessary, and begin to plan the next meeting. Some colleagues will not need to be reminded about what they have agreed to whereas others may benefit from questions on progress asked informally and others may need more overt support. As with so many other aspects of management, knowing your staff is essential and being flexible in your management style will pay dividends.

Some thoughts on chairing meetings

The success or failure of a meeting rests on how effectively the meeting is chaired. Usually, though not always, the team leader will be the person who chairs team meetings. The chairperson must fulfil a number of functions which make up the role. First, there is a leadership role. This involves setting guidelines, exercising authority, summarizing discussions, insisting on facts before opinions and countering limited vision that can come sometimes result from a group being well established and comfortable. Secondly, there is a gatekeeper role. This involves protecting the weak and vulnerable, encouraging the nervous, motivating the uninterested, controlling the dominant and managing ramblers and jokers. Thirdly, there is a referee role which involves keeping cool, staying neutral and managing conflict whilst at the same time allowing healthy debate. Finally, there is an administrative role which involves organizing the physical setting, keeping to time and ensuring notes are taken.

Effective chairing of meetings requires effective interpersonal skills. The chair must ensure that the atmosphere of the meeting is conducive to discussion and that members feel valued. Middle managers need to develop skills in managing teams during meetings. This means taking the lead, establishing acceptable behaviour and setting a good example. A sense of humour is very useful for diffusing conflict in a meeting and careful planning should avoid many problems. A middle manager who has created a good team ethos with a culture of support, cooperation and debate usually manages meetings well. There is an element of the chicken and the egg in this, however, as it is often well managed meetings that have contributed to a positive team spirit in the first place.

Sometimes it is beneficial to have a facilitator rather than a chairperson, depending on the purpose of the meeting. If the aim of the meeting is to generate ideas or problem-solve then a facilitator should be used. There are good reasons for the team leader not to be acting as facilitator and for a more neutral colleague to perform the role instead. It is almost impossible to run a fair, non-manipulative meeting when you have a personal investment in the subject matter. It is extremely difficult to lead a group objectively that is considering whether or not to discontinue a course that you introduced and have faith in, for example. Even if you try not to influence the group your body language is likely to reinforce those who hold the same views as you. Quite unintentionally, you might end up dominating the floor in your role as chairperson. A possible solution is to invite a fellow middle manager to act as a facilitator. They should, of course, have no preferences regarding outcomes of the meeting.

The facilitator needs to operate differently to a chairperson. They must be a neutral servant of the group and should not contribute or evaluate ideas. However, like a chairperson they must encourage all participants, protect individuals from personal attack and help the group arrive at a consensus. Facilitators make use of the following techniques to achieve their aims:

- flip charts for recording ideas;
- brainstorming;
- boomeranging questions back to group members;
- taking 'straw polls' to see if a line is worth pursuing;
- using 'negative voting' to see what options cannot be lived with;
- subdividing the group for discussions;
- using open questions;
- using rounds to hear what everyone thinks.

Some thoughts on seating

The arrangement of seats and tables sets the stage for a meeting and can influence what will happen. A circular pattern encourages a sense of warmth and togetherness. It is easy to make direct eye contact with everyone else and there is a sense of equality from the chair not being the focus of attention. The circle can be useful for informal discussions. However, whatever the mood of the group it will be heightened by the circle. If anger or aggression is in the air, this negative energy will be aimed directly at individuals and can lead to heavy encounters. If the pattern is an oval, one person's energy is focused on the person opposite and is thereby critically restricted. When everyone faces towards the person at the end of the table the collective energy is aimed at one individual, which is not conducive to problem-solving but is fine for a formal information giving session.

One of the most effective ways to get a group to focus on a task is to seat the participants in a semicircle facing the question written on a flip chart and facing the facilitator. The energy of the group is now directed towards the common problem. Ideally, the semi-circle should face away from the entrance to the room so that people coming in or leaving don't disrupt the flow of the meeting. The semi-circle is ideal for presentations and problem-solving sessions.

Reasons why meetings are unproductive

There are a number of common problems encountered in all kinds of meetings. Some of these problems can be solved by effective preparation and chairing, but others will only be remedied by building the kind of team culture that has been encouraged throughout this book. These problems include the following:

- everyone going off in different directions at the same time;
- attacks on individuals rather than their ideas;
- people finding it difficult to join the flow and participate;
- confusion over who is doing what in the meeting;
- abuse of power by chairperson to achieve personal objectives;
- too much information given in too short a time;
- going over the same old arguments again and again;
- lack of commitment from members, complacency or negativity;
- lack of clarity over objectives;
- hidden agendas;
- problem avoidance – 'everything's fine';

- people not listening to what is being said or only hearing what they want to hear;
- poor meeting environment – people can't hear, can't see, are too cold or too hot;
- lack of openness and trust.

Problem people

Some meetings are ineffective or have a negative feel because of the behaviour of particular individuals. Tight chairing will solve many problems but if certain people are persistently difficult it becomes necessary for the team leader to consider strategies for dealing with them individually. All participants of meetings display, at various times and in varying degrees, some of the following negative behaviour:

- arriving late and stopping the meeting so that they can catch up;
- leaving early and disrupting the flow of the meeting;
- popping in and out of a meeting to receive messages and phone calls;
- having only one thing to say and constantly repeating it;
- constantly putting new ideas down – 'that will never work';
- using non-verbal communication which is very dramatic – headshaking, rolling eyes, madly scribbling notes;
- contributing nothing and appearing totally disinterested or, worse still, engaging in a separate activity such as reading a book or marking;
- constantly whispering to a neighbour;
- talking too much and dominating a meeting;
- launching personal attacks on group members or the chair;
- interrupting what people are saying and rephrasing things for them;
- introducing gossip, anecdotes or rumours into a discussion;
- using status, qualifications or length of service to argue a point;
- telling the chair how to run the meeting.

It is important to think about how to deal with colleagues who are too shy to contribute in meetings, those who dominate meetings and those who are immature and distract others during meetings. Some basic tips are provided below.

- *Silent and shy colleagues* can be encouraged by having their achievements recognized. This builds self-esteem. The team leader should try and bring the shy person into discussions, perhaps by asking for comments on an area that is one of their strengths. Any contributions made during meetings should be rewarded with positive words and encouraging body language. As their confidence grows ask them to prepare a contribution on a topic that interests them and is relevant and provide feedback afterwards, in private of course. Sometimes discussion can be improved by subdividing a group and asking smaller clusters of people or pairs to report back to the whole group. A pair of shy people could be put together at these times. If a leader is deeply concerned by a person's lack of participation this should be discussed with them in private but done with sensitivity so that the shy person does not feel guilty about their lack of involvement.

- *Dominant and self-opinionated colleagues* can be given specific tasks to do that will prevent them dominating. Taking minutes is the obvious example. The use of subgroups during discussions could allow dominant people to be clustered together. Essentially, though, overbearing people need to be handled well by the chair who should insist on contributions being made through the chair and be assertive when self-opinionated people are dominating the meeting. This does not mean using put-downs but involves politely thanking them for their input and immediately bringing other people into the discussion before the dominant person continues with an argument or starts on a new point. Ultimately, encouraging everyone in a team to contribute and be assertive is the way forward. If dominant people are also aggressive managers need to discuss their behaviour with them in private.

- *Colleagues who 'clown around' and distract others* exist in some teams. They have a tendency to make light of serious issues by whispering to other colleagues or making inappropriate jokes. It is important to arrange seats in such a way that whispering becomes difficult and small groups cannot separate themselves from the main body. Analyse your reactions to the clowning to see if you are making the situation worse and reward positive contributions with praise. If necessary, establish ground rules for the conduct of meetings with the whole team and confront bad behaviour publicly. If it becomes necessary to address the behaviour through a private meeting do ensure that there is plenty of praise for the positive things this colleague contributes to the team.

It is worth remembering that bad behaviour in meetings is unusual and that managers who have cultivated a collaborative, open and positive culture rarely encounter difficulties in meetings. If team leaders feel the dynamics in a meeting are unproductive then it may be helpful to invite a trusted outside observer to watch a meeting and provide feedback that the whole team considers together with a view to improving matters.

1	Agenda received in advance	1	2	3	4	5	6
2	Meeting in suitable environment	1	2	3	4	5	6
3	Meeting kept to time	1	2	3	4	5	6
4	Documentation available	1	2	3	4	5	6
5	Decisions taken	1	2	3	4	5	6
6	Action points agreed	1	2	3	4	5	6
7	Participation of all team members	1	2	3	4	5	6
8	Appropriate leadership style adopted	1	2	3	4	5	6
9	Minutes clear and useful	1	2	3	4	5	6
10	Planning and review integral	1	2	3	4	5	6

1 = poor, 6 = excellent

Table 7.1   Meeting review chart

Reviewing your team meetings

Good managers reflect on all aspects of their practice. It is a good idea to find out from other team members what they think about the meetings you run. The Meeting Review Chart (Table 7.1) based on a design by James Sale (1998) could be used to provide feedback which could act as a basis for discussing meetings with others in the team and setting targets for improving meetings, if necessary.

Case study

Read the following comments and consider why the meeting in question was de-motivating for this participant.

Another meeting for Year 9 tutors this evening ... what a waste of time – the same old boring items. Why we have to sit and listen to Sue, the head of year, going through a catalogue of things she has had to deal with this week I don't know. She seems to assume we want to know about everything she's been doing; perhaps she just wants us to know what she does for the extra money she gets? I certainly get fed up of her moaning – I thought managers were supposed to be positive and full of optimism!

The arrangements for Open Evening are exactly the same as they were for the last one so why do we have to listen to them all over again. Surely she could have told Peter, a new tutor, about these at some other time. He was asking so many questions it must have wasted ten minutes.

I know I should take more interest but I'm not really bothered about what the new arrangements might be if we get the building extension. The LEA hasn't agreed yet so I can't really get enthusiastic about what might never happen anyway.

New job descriptions – that was an important item but Sue didn't give us any opportunity to discuss the matter. She'll probably land me with some extra responsibility – as if I don't have enough to do already. She also glossed over the issue of new admissions. There are now 32 students in my tutor group but I'm sure we have a policy of no more than 30 to a class. I think I'll have to ask the union rep about this as Sue was not very forthcoming.

To make matters worse it was freezing in the meeting room tonight but no-one dared to mention it – again. I suppose I should have said something if only to get it in the minutes. But then I never see the minutes so I wouldn't know for sure that Sue had put it in.

It was very embarrassing when Clive was asked to tell us about the drama work he'd thought of for his class. He obviously wasn't expecting to be asked to speak about it and he was quite coy at first. At least people showed some interest in what he was doing, which seemed to put him at his ease.

At the end of the meeting Sue asked if she could change next week's meeting to Tuesday. I felt really angry – she knows how difficult it is for me to change child-minding arrangements. It wouldn't be so bad if our meetings were productive! On my way out I passed my pigeonhole and found the agenda for the meeting I had just left. It must have been posted this afternoon as it was the first I'd seen of it. I screwed it up tight and ceremoniously tossed it in the bin to help relieve the tension I was feeling.

Reflection

This unfortunate teacher has a lot to feel annoyed about and it is not surprising she is feeling tense. Sue's handling of the meeting can be criticized on several grounds:
- The agenda was not provided in advance.
- The room was cold.
- Clive had not been warned about having to speak.
- Irrelevant items were included – Sue's work load and hypothetical building issues.
- Time was wasted answering questions for a new colleague who could have been seen at a different time.

- A major issue – admissions – was glossed over with no opportunity for discussion.
- Job descriptions were given out but not discussed – this should have been done with individuals on a one-to-one basis.
- The time of a scheduled meeting was changed at short notice.

Apart from failing to organize the meeting efficiently communication in general seems to be poor, members of Sue's team are not encouraged to assert themselves and there is certainly no culture of collaboration in evidence. However, colleagues were supportive and interested in what Clive had to say and they seem to cooperate with Sue despite the shoddy treatment meted out by her. From this short extract we can conclude that Sue lacks basic management skills and is failing to motivate, communicate and organize. Thankfully, there are probably few managers as incompetent as Sue in real life!

Summary

Productive, well-chaired meetings can help to create a purposeful team spirit and greatly increase the effectiveness of a department or group. Equally, badly organized and poorly focused meetings lower morale and sap energy. There are a range of reasons for holding meetings and team leaders need to be clear about what the purpose of holding a meeting is and then adopt a style which suits that purpose. An amusing way of understanding what makes an effective meeting is to consider what makes an ineffective meeting and then do the opposite. These are a few suggestions:

1. Never create an agenda – people might think about the issues in advance.
2. Be late for meetings – keeping people waiting is a clear sign of your importance.
3. Never discuss one topic fully when you can confuse people with several.
4. Don't hurry decisions – if you wait long enough the problem might go away.
5. Don't have relevant papers to hand – you can all sit and wait for the photocopier.
6. Run long meetings and invite people for whom the issues are irrelevant.
7. Meet regularly when there is nothing to do.
8. Don't get things too clear, e.g. what has been decided – then you have a good reason for holding another meeting.

9. Don't set a finish time – people have nothing else to do and the head is sure to be impressed by the long hours your team puts in.
10. Take phone calls during the meeting – it shows how much in demand you are.

- *Daily list.* Have a list of jobs to do for each day. Ticking them off as you go along will give you a great sense of satisfaction. As new things crop up note them on your list; don't rely on your memory!
- *Filing cabinet.* Always file away important information and ruthlessly discard unimportant pieces of paper. Go through your filing cabinet once a term and remove information that is no longer relevant. An efficient filing system should allow you to find things in seconds rather than minutes and should be able to be easily understood by others. If you fall ill colleagues will need to be able to lay their hands on papers that are normally your responsibility. Make sure your filing system enables them to do this.
- *Computer.* Use and develop your computer skills. Many aspects of administration can be made easier with a computer. Handbooks can easily be updated, class lists can easily be revised, pupils' marks can be stored efficiently and so on. If you use a home computer, try and make sure it is compatible with your school system. Carry information on floppy discs so that you can work on files at home or at work but always remember to update information on both systems. Use file names which will not confuse you when you want to access information. Remember there is legislation concerning the holding of pupil information on computer so check out your school's policy with the senior member of staff responsible.
- *Current folder.* Hold documents that you are working on in a *current folder.* Items should not remain in the current folder for more than a couple of weeks.
- *Highlighter.* When you first read a document highlight key words and ideas. This will help you to process it much more quickly or to focus on the important parts if you have to return to it.
- *Waste bin.* A lot of what comes into your pigeonhole will be irrelevant. You will be able to tell very quickly if something really is of no interest or is irrelevant. File such items in the bin. Do not become the kind of middle manager whose desk is covered with several piles of catalogues, circulars and out-of-date memos. A cluttered desk is usually a sign of poor decision-making.
- *The first hour of the working day.* If your domestic arrangements allow, arrive at work in time to deal with routine administration. It is amazing just how much you can get done before the pupils arrive. Teachers who arrive only a few minutes before the children often seem disorganized and look harassed. Feeling organized really does help your performance. If you are unable to arrive early use your weekly planner to build in regular time slots for dealing with routine matters.

Managing resources

In the broadest sense the resources which have to be managed by team leaders include people, time, money and equipment/materials. Managing people has been addressed in earlier chapters and time management is considered in Chapter 11. The management of money and materials will be considered in this section. Money refers to the team's budget or *capitation* (the amount allocated from the school budget to your area for teaching equipment/materials). Teaching equipment/materials can include textbooks, stationery, paper, photocopies, videos, AV equipment, computers, software and more. Materials which need reordering yearly or termly because they are used up in the process of delivering the curriculum (for example, exercise books, paper, glue) are known as *consumables*.

Day-to-day resource management

Every day in schools a wide range of equipment and materials is used. The ease and efficiency with which individual teachers can gain access to the resources they need can have a very significant impact on their morale and on the learning of children in their care. A five-minute wait at the start of a lesson while a video and TV are located and set up is five minutes of learning time wasted; a lesson planned around a set of textbooks which are then not available is likely to result in a very unproductive teaching session.

Team leaders must, therefore, devise a system for resource management that is both efficient and effective. A system will only work if it is adhered to by all colleagues. This is more likely to happen if colleagues have been involved in decisions about the system. Maverick behaviour should not be tolerated; individual teachers who hoard resources for themselves or hide sets of textbooks should be challenged. Equally, teachers who forget to return resources or who do not look after sets of books should be gently reminded that they are inconveniencing their colleagues, even if unintentionally. Getting the team ethos right is really important. If team members are respectful and supportive of each other and realize how their behaviour impacts on other colleagues (or, to use TQM terminology, see colleagues as 'internal clients') then they are less likely to be uncooperative about making an agreed system for managing resources work. Of course, the team leader must set the tone by ensuring that they don't abuse their position by always appearing to have the best resources, teaching rooms and so on.

It is not easy to advocate a particular system for resource management because all schools are very different in terms of buildings and organization. A department with a suite of purpose-built rooms, a department office and a large storeroom will be able to organize things very differently to a department housed in a number of temporary buildings away from the main school and with no office facility. In some schools AV equipment is held in a Resources Centre whereas in others departments possess their own AV equipment.

However, there are certain basic questions to ask when deciding on a storage system for the resources belonging to your department or team:

- How often will this resource be used? The more often it is used the more accessible it should be.
- Who needs to be able to use this resource? The more people who need access to a resource the more open its method of storage should be.
- For how long should we keep resources? Be ruthless about throwing out old resources. Storage space in most schools is limited and there is no point in keeping redundant resources in the hope that they might come in 'handy' one day.
- Who will be responsible for managing the storage of this resource? Remember, the team leader should not necessarily be responsible for all resources but all resources do need somebody to look after them.

When you have identified teaching resources which are regularly used by several team members, questions need to be asked about possible locations:

- Can people get it without disturbing someone's lesson?
- Can it be reached without shifting other things?
- If sheets, are they kept in files, boxes or a filing cabinet?
- If textbooks, can they easily be transported from room to room? Remember health and safety may be an issue here.
- If AV equipment, is the location secure and safe?
- Does the choice of location inconvenience some colleagues more than others?
- Who will keep track of resources? How?

Budgeting

Middle managers, especially heads of department and heads of faculty, are responsible for spending a proportion of the school's budget. It is important that your share of the school's capitation is spent efficiently and in such a way that spending is related to your development plan, which in turn is designed to provide the best possible education for the children in your care. You will need to be able to account for the money you spend.

There are three main elements to this task:
1. linking the funds available to priorities identified in your development plan;
2. keeping a record of the way money is spent and balancing the books;
3. evaluating the effectiveness of your spending.

These elements are linked to the development planning process described in Chapter 9 and illustrated in Figure 8.1.

Gaining funds for development priorities

There is a chicken and egg situation with regard to linking funds to development priorities. Will your priorities be determined by the funds you know you will receive or should your priorities determine the funds you receive? There is no simple answer but most schools settle for a compromise. A set amount of capitation is provided to teams determined by a figure per pupil being multiplied by the number of pupils taught by a particular department. There is usually a *weighting* included which means that practical subjects (which use more consumables) and sixth-form groups (usually smaller in number than lower-school groups) receive a higher figure per pupil. On top of this basic allowance, there is usually a pot of money to

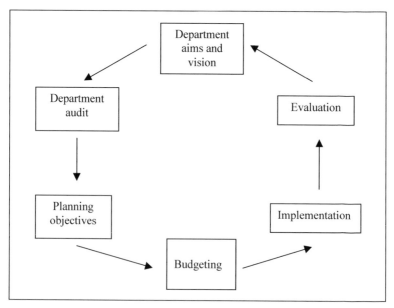

Figure 8.1   Linking development planning and budgeting

bid for. This allows teams introducing new courses or approaches to present their case for additional funding. Obviously, money in most schools is very tight and so bids for additional money are only likely to succeed if the changes they finance meet one or more of the following criteria:

- The proposed change is a response to legislation.
- The proposed change is in line with the school's strategic plan and current development plan priorities.
- The proposed change is a response to market research findings (for example, the introduction of a new A-level course which is not currently offered with the result that many Year 11 students choose to attend other sixth forms where the course is offered).
- The proposed change will lead to measurable improvements in pupil performance.
- The proposed change is in response to the findings of inspection by OFSTED.

Clearly, a bid has to be professionally presented and realistic if it is to be taken seriously. The following points give an idea of the kind of information you should include in your bid for additional funds.

- A rationale for your proposed change or spending. This will probably have emerged from the audit process (see Chapter 9).
- How the proposal relates to school development plan priorities.
- Clear objectives relating to your proposal.
- An indication of how the effectiveness of the proposed spending might be measured. Can you produce hard targets? For example, if you want to spend on new textbooks so that all students in examination groups can take a book home do you expect an improvement in homework submission, course work marks or exam results? Can the improvements expected be quantified?
- Very clear costings for materials, reprographics and INSET as appropriate. Can you show that you have 'shopped around' to get the best prices on materials and books?

Records of spending

As a middle manager it should not be necessary for you to keep detailed accounts. There will be school administrators paid to do this. However, you need to keep track of your planned and actual spending during a financial year and also keep an accurate record of incomings and outgoings relating to school trips etc. You may be required to produce such records for school auditors.

The easiest way to keep track of spending is to use an order book or file. Design a simple grid sheet using the following headings for columns:

- Date (the date the order was placed);
- Received (tick this column when items ordered have been received);
- Details (include the supplier's name, catalogue reference number and brief description of the order);
- Estimated cost;
- Actual cost as invoiced (this may include price changes, postage and packing etc.);
- Balance (use pencil to write the balance based on estimated cost and then use pen to enter when actual cost is known).

As part of the development planning audit include a financial review. Money is always scarce so it is worth discussing with colleagues how economies might be made. Here are some important questions to ask:

- Can we save on exercise books and paper? In many schools A4 paper is given out very freely or pupils simply help themselves with the result that the paper bill becomes a very significant part of a department's budget.
- Can we reduce expenditure on textbook replacement? In some schools there is a tremendous loss of textbooks each year with a very high cost attached. There is a big difference between having to replace old textbooks and having to replace books because teachers have not kept accurate records of which pupils have borrowed books.
- Can we reduce our photocopying bill? Photocopying is expensive and should be avoided except in emergencies or when only single copies of papers are needed. Most schools have less expensive reprographic facilities and colleagues should be organized enough to be able to take advantage of these and have worksheets done in advance by a technician. It is also poor use of a teacher's time to be standing at a photocopier. Departments should avoid getting themselves into a situation where worksheets have become a substitute for textbooks. This may save money in the short term but becomes very costly in the long run.
- Can we reduce our spending on consumables? Far too often items such as pencils and rulers are ordered year after year because pupils have stolen them. While some loss is almost inevitable teachers should be determined to check that things are not going missing in their lessons. If all team members are determined to reduce the loss of consumables pupils will soon get the message.

Stock control

Managers of well-run departments know what resources are available to assist the teaching and learning process and make sure that colleagues also know what resources there are.

A stock book should be kept listing non-consumable resources in the department, including serial numbers in the case of items of electrical equipment (useful if equipment is stolen or insurance claims have to be made). All textbooks, slides, computer software and videotapes should be fully catalogued with reference to which year groups and courses they are appropriate for. Schemes of work will, of course, contain reference to key resources. Numbers of each set of textbooks should be recorded and numbers checked at least once a term. Individual books within sets should be given a number. These numbers can then be entered into teachers' record books when books are lent out to pupils. In this way responsibility for looking after resources is passed to pupils. Those who lose books should, as a rule, be charged the cost of a replacement. This helps to make pupils take looking after books seriously.

Videotapes should be numbered so that they are easy to locate. If certain programmes are used regularly and the same video player is likely to be used note down the number displayed on the video counter and write it on the tape so that colleagues save time when trying to locate a programme. Just as considerate teachers clean the board they have used ready for the next teacher so rewinding a tape to the start of a programme is a helpful thing to do. Encourage colleagues to be helpful in this way. When a tape is full remove the tab so that it cannot be recorded over by accident. Have a booking system in operation for TV/video and other AV equipment so that colleagues are not planning lessons to include equipment that is unavailable.

Regarding consumables, it is likely that you will be ordering a similar amount of staple items such as exercise books and paper each year (unless significant economies can be made). Save a copy of each year's stationery order, so that you are not starting from scratch each time you put in an order.

Case studies

Outlined below are two extreme examples of how heads of department manage their GCSE textbooks. Read the cases studies and then reflect on the advantages and disadvantages of each approach.

Study 1

Greg Smith has been head of History for two years. He is a dynamic teacher but doesn't like administration. He is good at praising colleagues but feels uneasy about tackling them when things are not going as well as they should. He asks his two fellow GCSE teachers to keep a record of textbooks lent out to students each year.

However, he has found that during the two years he has been in post almost a third of the copies of the core GCSE textbook have been 'lost' and the expense of replacing these each year has punched a large hole in the department's budget. As his colleagues are hardworking he feels reluctant to challenge them about the lost books. He is also embarrassed by the fact that some of his own students have failed to return books and he has not followed this up. As the books are kept in the departmental storeroom and all teachers have access to them he has no accurate record of which colleagues lose most books. He is convinced that part of the problem is allowing students to keep textbooks for revision right up to the day of the GCSE exam but he is reluctant to deprive students of this facility.

Study 2

Marian Small has been head of History for twenty years. She is a rigid and traditional teacher and has developed a system for the use of GCSE textbooks which she insists her two GCSE colleagues use. Pupils and teachers alike know exactly where they stand with regard to books but both have their moans about the rigidity of the system and about Marian's policing of it. The system is this: There are enough textbooks for all GCSE pupils. These are divided into three sets, one for each group. All three sets are stored in Miss Small's room. Each book in a set is numbered. Each student knows their number. At the start of each lesson a group monitor collects the books and gives them out. At the end of each lesson they are collected in and returned to Miss Small. No books are allowed home – over the years Miss Small has created a number of worksheets which are used for homework. Some parents have complained about children not having a GCSE textbook at home but there have been major rows with colleagues who have 'broken the rules' by allowing books out of school. Over the years virtually no textbooks have been lost and hardly any contain graffiti. They are only replaced when, because of old age, they begin to fall to pieces.

Reflection

Both heads of History have their good points and bad points as do their approaches to textbooks.

Clearly, Miss Small's system ensures that books are not lost and this makes money available for other things. Providing homework has been clearly thought out not allowing books home will not necessarily be a problem. However, time is wasted at the beginning and end of lessons and 'catching up' may be difficult for students who have been absent. Miss Small's approach is likely to upset staff as it suggests they are not to be trusted and by allowing no flexibility at all it undermines colleagues who may have very good reasons for allowing exceptions to the rule. The system is so 'over the top' it suggests that Miss Small has got her priorities wrong as a head of department.

Greg Smith does not really have a system at all and this is the root of the problem in his department. There is no individual accountability as everyone has access to all the books. Colleagues are asked to ensure books are not lost but this is not monitored. As lost books are replaced each year there is no incentive to reduce the annual loss. On the plus side Greg's heart is in the right place: he loves teaching, he wants the pupils to have every opportunity to prepare for exams using textbooks and he is keen to keep his team happy and motivated. It seems that Greg has not yet made the transition from teacher to team leader; yet with hardworking staff, discussing the problem of book wastage and agreeing a new approach which can be monitored should not be a problem.

Loss of books is an issue facing all departments in all secondary schools. In effective teams a system midway between the two extremes outlined above is likely to exist. Fewer books are likely to be lost if:

- individual teachers have control of a set of books rather than several teachers sharing a set;
- individual pupils have their own textbook and are responsible for it;
- pupils who lose or damage books are made to pay for a replacement;
- team leaders take the monitoring of stock seriously and investigate unacceptable levels of loss;
- team members discuss the issue of book wastage and agree on a policy which is easy to operate and is fair to all pupils.

Summary

Some of the points made in this chapter may seem very divorced from the vision creating and team building covered earlier in this book. They are actually closely connected. Good management is about being able to see the future and wider picture but also deal with the present and the nuts and bolts of day-to-day organization. Of course, an *obsession* with the nuts and bolts is not healthy and may indicate that a team leader has got his or her priorities wrong. However, a middle manager who can help colleagues do a good job by having efficient systems for day-to-day organization in place will gain much respect.

You will feel more organized if you are able to develop an approach to administration that is disciplined and does not allow paperwork to become the tail that wags the dog. Effective use of your diary and planner, ruthlessness over discarding much of the paper that appears in your pigeonhole and developing working patterns which include slots for attending to paperwork are all important strategies for dealing with administration.

The day-to-day running of your department will be enhanced if you are able to develop systems for the fair and efficient use of resources. Easy access to materials and books, an efficient booking system for TV and other equipment and delegating responsibility for checking resources are all important. With regard to finance, ensuring that colleagues are committed to limiting photocopying, preventing loss of consumables and ensuring all books are accounted for will help to free up money for providing other things that team members feel are needed. This identification of needs should be linked to the development planning cycle and should involve all team members.

Finally, never lose sight of the fact that effective administration and resource management are not ends in themselves. They are important for helping you and your team to achieve the more important goals of providing a good education for your pupils and raising their levels of achievement. 'A meaningful life is not a matter of speed or efficiency. It's much more a matter of what you do and why you do it, than how fast you get it done' (Covey 1994). This observation should make just as much sense when applied to management in schools.

CHAPTER NINE

Managing Change and Development

Introduction

The current reform agenda for schools in England and Wales has had a more profound impact than even the transformation that occurred in our secondary schools following comprehensivization in the mid-1960s. The determination of successive governments to drive up pupil achievement and make schools more accountable has resulted in wave upon wave of centrally directed initiatives being implemented in schools. This 'top-down' approach to change has produced some improvements in those things which can easily be measured but, arguably, has created in some schools a kind of innovation fatigue and has left many teachers feeling de-skilled, mere technicians following the instructions of those on high.

Despite a heavily deterministic national agenda effective schools and departments still feel that they can shape educational provision in their own way and can control change rather than be controlled by it. Such schools use the impetus of external reform to improve or develop themselves. Sometimes what they do is consistent with the national reform agenda, sometimes they introduce change because of particular circumstances unique to their situations. In these cases what is best for young people in that school or department is always the driving force. Schools with the following features have been identified as most likely to manage change effectively:

- trust, openness and collaboration;
- clear underlying values and beliefs;
- good staff–student relationships.

Holly and Southworth (1989) see the culture of 'developing' schools as enabling, promoting learning and growth for adult members as well as students. They describe the culture as 'interactive and negotiative; creative and problem-solving; proactive and responsive; participative and collaborative; flexible and challenging; risk-taking and enterprising; evaluative and reflective; supportive and developmental' (Holly and Southworth 1989).

Change can be threatening and unsettling and can cause weariness and fatigue. Equally, introducing change can be an opportunity for learning, creativity and personal development. Effective management can make the difference between a cynical and lack-lustre approach to change and an approach characterized by enthusiasm and commitment. Middle managers play a vital role in the change process and their level of success in managing change will be dependent upon good inter-personal skills, a collaborative team culture and effective planning. The importance of middle managers in directing change is detailed under 'Strategic direction and development of the subject' in *National Standards for Subject Leaders* (TTA 1998).

School development and the change process

It is important that managers understand how change affects the individual. All change causes a certain amount of stress to the individual but it will not necessarily always be negative stress. The extent to which a change is *desired* and *predicted* determines how stressful it will be. For example, taking up a new post can be stressful. This is because you are moving from what Plant (1987) calls 'firm ground' to 'swampy ground'. You are stepping out of a position where you feel confident, you understand the culture and your role is clear into an altogether more uncomfortable position where you are uncertain about your role, relationships and responsibilities. However, because the new job was desired and success in securing the post boosted your self-esteem you will probably turn the stress into creative energy and work very hard to make a success of the post.

There are other occasions, of course, where change that was not expected or desired can cause great stress which, at least in the short term, can lead to loss of self-esteem, decline in performance and depression. It is clear from this that managers need to involve colleagues fully in decisions about change and the change process. Change should not be seen as undesirable or unexpected and the greater the involvement of team members in decisions about the future the less likely it is that change will have a negative effect on them. This is why a collaborative culture usually produces smooth and effective change.

Everyone has a need for a certain amount of stability, either personal or professional. The stress factors of moving house, getting married or getting divorced are well documented. A teacher experiencing stress outside work will be unlikely to embrace change in the workplace with enthusiasm. By recognizing the need for some stability managers can show understanding and provide support. People come from different backgrounds with different experiences and therefore cope with change in different ways and at differing speeds. Managers need to acknowledge this when change is being introduced.

> When those who have the power to manipulate changes act as if they have only to explain, and, when their explanations are not at once accepted, shrug off opposition as ignorance or prejudice, they express a profound contempt for the meaning of lives other than their own. (Marris 1975)

Of course, middle managers cannot control the speed of change that is centrally imposed but they can make the change less threatening by providing support for colleagues and by ensuring that the change is controlled, directed and shared. When a collaborative and supportive culture exists in a team change can usually be accomplished smoothly. Indeed, in most successful schools bottom-up change is common, with discussion and the implementation of new ideas and ways of improving provision seen as quite normal.

Even so, change in schools ultimately concerns changes in individual practice, which some colleagues find more difficult to cope with than others do. It is likely that the implementation of a significant curriculum or organizational change will involve one or more of the following features:

- changes in the structure and organization of the school; for example timetabling or the shape of the school day;
- new or additional teaching materials; for example PCs in the classroom;
- teachers acquiring new knowledge, resulting from curriculum changes, for example;
- teachers adopting new ways of working; for example moving away from a didactic style to resource-based learning;
- changes in beliefs or values on the part of some teachers, the introduction of GNVQ or the introduction of streaming for example.

A fear of change or simply a desire to avoid the additional work generated by change can produce an initial reluctance to embrace a new idea from even the most dedicated teachers. In certain circumstances, though, opposition to change may be more pronounced. Hall and Oldroyd (1990) note that in settings where staff response to new initiatives was poor:

- morale is low;
- change agents are not respected;
- there is a track record of failed innovation;
- risk-taking is discouraged;
- leaders are inflexible in their attitude;
- there is little outside support.

Managing development

Managing development in schools involves controlling and directing change in order to improve the service and nature of education provided. In turbulent times a clear sense of direction and routes to follow are essential and effective development planning should provide these. Development planning is now well established in just about all state schools with middle managers being actively involved in the process and critical to its success. According to Hargreaves and Hopkins (1991) the merits of development planning are as follows.

- It focuses attention on the aims of education.
- It provides a coordinated approach to change.
- It considers long-term vision and short-term goals.
- It puts control of change into the hands of teachers.
- Staff development becomes more focused.
- The achievements of teachers in promoting change are recognized.
- It becomes easier to report on the work of the school.

Schools should have a strategic plan, a school development plan, departmental and team development plans and programme plans (see Figure 9.1). Together, these plans help schools to provide answers to several important questions:

- Where is the school now? (audit)
- Where do we want it to be in five years' time? (vision)
- What changes do we need to make? (construction)
- How shall we manage these changes? (implementation)
- How shall we know whether our management of change has been successful? (evaluation)

A strategic plan communicates decisions that have been agreed concerning the long-term (usually five years) development of the school. The strategic plan reflects the values, vision, mission, aims and policies of the school. These will shape the planning goals for the future.

A school development plan prioritizes a limited number of goals from the strategic plan. It contains a range of mandatory and discretionary goals. Typically, action points from OFSTED inspections form the basis for development plans but they are not driven exclusively by OFSTED. Internal audits and external market research might also shape a school development plan. According to Hopkins and MacGilchrist (1998) schools are increasingly using their development plans as a means of raising student achievement through focusing on the quality of teaching and learning. Development plans are often written in detail for the forthcoming year and in outline for the two following years. This three-year rolling plan approach helps to provide a balance between short- and medium-term planning.

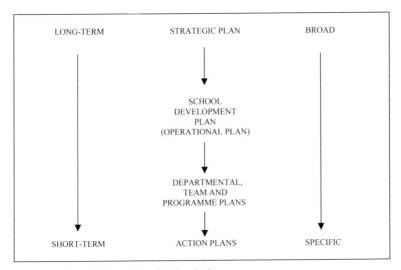

Figure 9.1   A hierarchy of school plans

Departmental and team development plans will be strongly influenced by the school's strategic plan, by school development plan priorities and by OFSTED inspection findings. However, teams and departments may have areas for development that they themselves have identified and regard as important.

Programme plans may be written by small teams of people or by individuals. They are usually concerned with the implementation of inter-disciplinary programmes, possibly developed by working parties. Programme plans on 'Staff Appraisal' or 'Recording and Reporting' are two examples.

Action plans turn the first year of the development plan or programme plan into a working document for teachers. Action plans describe and summarize what needs to be done to implement and evaluate key priorities. They clarify what has to be done by assigning responsibility for action. Action plans show:
- targets to be achieved in implementing a particular goal;
- resources allocated;
- individuals responsible;
- completion dates;
- success criteria.

The action plan is thus a convenient guide to action. The better the quality of the action plan, the more likely it is that implementation will proceed smoothly. The more effectively all team members can be involved in drawing up the action plan the more likely it is to succeed.

Making a success of team development planning

Middle managers can achieve smooth and successful change by creating a collaborative team culture in which individuals are constantly striving to improve the education they provide and by using well-established development planning techniques. Team leaders operate within a wider school development planning context and so a clear understanding of the whole-school approach to development planning is important.

The development planning cycle

Essentially, development planning is a cyclical process that involves audit, construction, implementation and evaluation. In most secondary schools the audit and construction phases occur during the summer term when there is usually the opportunity for teams to spend more time together. Implementation usually takes place during the autumn and spring terms. Evaluation should be ongoing but with a more thorough evaluation at the end of the cycle, in the late spring term, which feeds into the audit. It is obviously the case that raising pupil achievement is a major aim, whatever the specific development plan targets, and an analysis of external exam results should occur in September and be revisited at the audit stage of the cycle.

It is, of course, impossible to address every issue which might require attention in a development plan. Development planning involves making decisions about which issues take priority, which areas will be maintained and which will be developed (see Figure 9.2). Highly successful schools and departments are likely to include more maintenance and fine-tuning than new initiatives in their development plans. However, education operates in a rapidly changing world and it is unlikely that any team will ever be in a position where no change is necessary and no improvement is possible.

The audit

The audit stage is extremely important and involves a review of strengths and weaknesses. It provides a good opportunity for team building with openness, reflection and constructive criticism being essential. The audit should be seen as an evaluative summary of the team's performance in the key areas of its work. The key areas of its work should be defined in relation to pupil performance, national legislation and whole-school aims and mission. The audit should involve evidence gained from the evaluation stage of the development planning cycle and from other

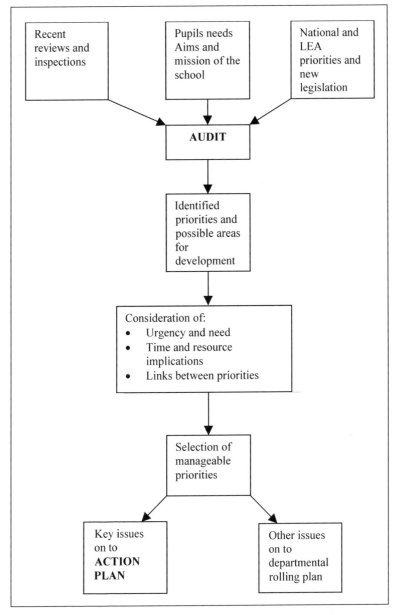

Figure 9.2 Construction of the departmental development plan

evidence available such as exam results, SATS results and the findings of OFSTED inspections.

It is also very useful to think about conducting market research to assist with the audit process. Increasingly, pupils' opinions are being used to assist team leaders in making judgements about the quality of education that they provide. While some teachers are horrified by the idea of students assessing them others are beginning to accept the notion of 'child as client'. Teams where openness exists and colleagues are supportive are more likely to consider using student assessments as part of the evaluation and audit process. We all know that at options time the pupils make judgements about courses and teachers by voting with their feet. We often become aware through anecdotal evidence of what the views of pupils are but the picture we get is a partial one. Investigating pupils' attitudes in a more systematic way, therefore, would seem sensible and the information gathered, if used sensitively, could help teams to consider how best to improve their practice. It could be used to inform decisions on curriculum and pedagogy and also for individual staff reviews and appraisals.

A departmental audit involves consideration of strengths and weaknesses of the department but it isn't possible to conduct a *detailed* audit of every aspect of a team's work every year. A balance has to be reached between reviewing areas of provision which relate to whole-school development initiatives and reviewing aspects of provision because the team or team leader believes it is important to do so. Workload is a major consideration and it is important to be realistic; attempting to do too much in any one year is likely to result in frustration if ambitious plans are not achieved.

The audit should involve answering such questions as:
- What are we doing well?
- What are we not happy with?
- What statutory requirements and LEA policies affect us?
- What are the constraints?
- What are the opportunities?
- What should we try and change over the next year?
- What should we try and change over the next three years?

Performance indicators

A performance indicator is a piece of information that helps you to know how well a person, group or organization is performing. It is important to include performance indicators in the audit process. SATS, GCSE and A-level results can be useful, especially when they are analysed to indicate 'value added' scores for your subject. Increasingly, schools are using sophisticated measures to establish how well they are performing compared with other schools catering for pupils of similar ability and backgrounds.

Quantitative performance indicators by themselves rarely provide definitive answers but they do help teams to focus on the important questions to ask. They draw attention to issues that deserve a closer look. Comparisons between one year and another, between subjects, between teachers of the same subject and with local and national norms help to focus teams on the key question: are we doing the best we can for our pupils?

Middle managers must be committed to raising achievement in schools. The sensitive use of statistical information on pupil performance with teams and individuals can be a useful part of this process. However, if such performance indicators are used to blame and shame individual teachers it is likely that the collaborative and supportive culture that is so important for achieving success will be undermined. 'Total quality management does not seek to attribute blame, total quality management seeks to understand and control quality' (Smith 1996). Analysing pupil performance in exams is likely to become increasingly important with the legal requirement (set out in Circular 11/98) for governing bodies to set targets for pupils' achievement in terms of the percentage of pupils gaining A*–C grades at GCSE level. It is also likely that in the future a more rigorous form of teacher appraisal will emerge linked to some form of performance-related pay.

The development plan and the action plan

Once the audit has been conducted it is possible to translate the findings into a development plan or rolling plan and an action plan. Establishing priorities, and an order for dealing with them, is the way a team can control change rather than be controlled by it.

When choosing between priorities in order to decide which issues should be dealt with urgently (action plan) and which should be addressed in the coming years the following questions are important.

Urgency
- What is unavoidable (e.g. a legal requirement)?
- What are the consequences of delay?
- Will it wait or will things get worse?

Manageability
- Can the development be achieved in a manageable time-scale or should tasks be subdivided?

- Have we got the resources to achieve the task?
- Do we need outside support?

Roots and branches
- Have we got the right philosophy, team structure and team skills to make the change work (the roots)?
- Are the changes needed a natural extension of what we have already started (the branches)?

Links
- Are priorities inter-related?
- Will tackling one make it easier to address another?

Answering these questions will help a team arrive at an action plan. Action plans should capture long-term vision in manageable short-term goals. Action plans should set out specific success criteria, identify group and individual responsibilities and completion dates. Action plans state realistic targets to be achieved within a given time. Using a format such as the one provided in Table 9.1 helps to make action plan decisions easily accessible to team members and to senior managers and outside agencies.

When aiming to achieve complex objectives or where developments involve inter-related elements, it is important to undertake a critical path analysis. This involves agreeing a timetable for action and listing on it deadlines relevant to each stage of the proposed development. Summarizing these on a grid which shows the months of the year, individual deadlines and who is responsible helps to improve the management of development.

Success criteria

Success criteria used in development planning should relate to specific targets. They should be capable of demonstrating that targets have been achieved. They should be used by teams during the review and audit stages of development planning in order to evaluate success.

Of course, some success criteria will be more easily measured than others. If an objective is to rewrite a Year 9 scheme of work then the new document will provide clear evidence that the target has been achieved. If another target is to increase uptake of a subject at GCSE level then the numbers of pupils taking the subject compared with previous years may be used as success criteria. However, in this case demonstrating cause and effect may be more difficult. In order to recruit more students to GCSE classes you may have modified your Year 9 courses to generate more

Action Plan Summary		Team/Dept.		Date				
Start date	Objective(s) Target(s)	Action needed	Person responsible	Assisted by	Resources, INSET and costs	Success criteria	Completion date

Table 9.1 Action plan summary sheet

interest, marketed your subject more actively at option time and introduced a newsletter for your subject. Which of these initiatives produced the increase in students opting for your subject will be difficult to establish. Indeed, it is possible that other subjects becoming less attractive rather than yours becoming more desirable caused the change. Conversely, introducing the new initiatives in Year 9 aimed at increasing uptake may have been achieved (for example, there may have been a wonderful newsletter produced) but may not have had the desired effect of increasing uptake. This illustrates the difficulty involved in deciding on success criteria. It also warns us of the dangers of always seeking to demonstrate success in terms of only what is measurable in statistical terms.

Keeping developments on track

After the audit and construction stages of the development planning cycle are complete it is important not to assume that agreed action will simply progress on auto-pilot. Successful implementation needs support and sustaining commitment is a key task for team leaders. The enthusiasm of even the most competent and committed teachers can wane simply because of the pressures of everyday teaching.

There are simple but effective ways in which middle managers can keep things on track. First, an occasional, informal enquiry about progress to a teacher demonstrates that their efforts are appreciated and provides them with an opportunity to raise with you any difficulties they are encountering. Secondly, having progress reviews built into some departmental meetings means that individuals with responsibility for action will have to report the progress they have made to colleagues. This helps to prevent complacency and again provides an opportunity for identifying difficulties being encountered. Thirdly, an enlarged copy of the development plan summary should be displayed on your team notice board with targets achieved ticked or crossed out so that everyone has an idea of the progress being made.

If things are not proceeding to plan it is usually because time schedules are too tight, circumstances have changed, unexpected obstacles have been encountered or key colleagues have simply allowed matters to drift. Progress checks allow re-orientation to take place. Where a collaborative team culture exists, most problems can easily be overcome. If a major obstacle has emerged which the team was unaware of at the time of constructing the development plan it may be necessary to modify your targets. However, this should only be done if absolutely necessary.

Techniques for generating team involvement

Successful development planning depends to a great extent on staff commitment and involvement. Much of this book has been devoted to the effective management of individuals and teams and the creation of a 'can-do' culture. The audit stage of development planning provides a great opportunity for a team to clarify its aims and philosophy and work together on deciding how the education you are providing can be improved. However, in a team where all members are not yet committed to the idea of continuous improvement or where teachers are simply suffering innovation fatigue generating interest in further development becomes a real challenge to middle managers. The key is to create opportunities for staff involvement so that they feel ownership of the development plan. The imposition of change can never be as effective as the embracing of change.

Brainstorming is one way of generating involvement (see Chapter 5) and *process analysis* is another. This is a group problem-solving approach used for examining the operation of a process or procedure in order to identify ways in which it can be improved. Inducting Year 7 pupils, guiding Year 9 pupils at option time, preparing Year 11 for exams and organizing field trips are all examples of *services* that might be improved by process analysis. The benefits of the technique are that it fosters collaboration, it increases commitment and it helps a team to develop a coherent view of a complex process.

The technique is similar to preparing a flow chart and involves the group in critical review by: mapping the main stages in the process; detailing what happens at each stage; evaluating each stage of the process; and agreeing strategies for improvement. Process analysis needs to be conducted in an atmosphere free from blame and where everyone's opinions are considered. The team should sit in a horseshoe shape facing a wall. Recording ideas on large sheets of paper on the wall means that the information is clear and all can see it. Diversions and side-tracking become obvious and are likely to be corrected by the group. Individuals can see easily how they contribute to the whole process under review. By increasing understanding greater collaboration during implementation can be achieved.

When auditing the work of a team a *SWOT analysis* should be conducted, involving all team members. SWOT stands for strengths, weaknesses, opportunities and threats and it is a useful technique for summing up the status of your department or team in both a school and a national context. It helps a team to look to the future and avoid complacency. The team leader must prepare for the analysis by producing key questions that raise awareness of school and national issues.

Reflection: evaluating your department

A *departmental review survey* is an excellent device for contributing to the review and audit stage of a department's development planning cycle. A possible survey is provided as Table 9.2 and, at the time of writing, a survey on which Table 9.2 is based is available on the internet free of charge (www.hod.org.uk).

The survey should be completed and handed in confidentially. Participants should be encouraged to use the whole range of scores available and not restrict themselves to 3s and 4s. When all the sheets are returned the scores can be averaged to produce two rankings: one on the basis of 'importance' (column A) and one on the basis of 'performance' (column B). Each descriptor can then be placed into one of four categories:

- *Those high in both importance and performance rankings.* These areas of success can be celebrated and analysed to see if the reasons for success can be replicated in other areas.
- *Those high in importance but low in performance.* These issues will need to be considered for inclusion in the development plan.
- *Those low in importance but high in performance.* These issues might be unpopular 'housekeeping' tasks or irritating time wasters. It is important to consider which is the case.
- *Those low in both importance and performance.* These can probably be ignored.

Summary

'The purpose of development planning is to improve the quality of teaching and learning in a school through successful management of innovation and change' (Hargreaves and Hopkins 1991). Middle managers are critical to the success of school development. By being systematic in their approach to development planning they can help to reduce the stress associated with change and can ensure that the aims and mission of a school are translated into practice through 'a logical progression from policy formulation to policy implementation within the planning hierarchy' (Giles 1997).

Heads of department and heads of year will principally be involved in the writing of development plans and action plans for their areas. These form part of the school development plan and contain targets relating to whole-school aims as well as targets generated by the team relating to issues of concern that they have identified.

Departmental review survey

Relative Personal Priority (A)	Reflects this Department (B)
1 = Top priority	1= Strongly agree
2 = High priority	2 = Agree
3 = Fairly important	3 = Slightly agree
4 = Not really important	4 = Slightly disagree
5 = Low priority	5 = Disagree
6 = Lowest priority	6 = Strongly disagree

Number	Criterion	A	B
1	Schemes of work are agreed by the department as a whole		
2	Tasks are delegated fairly		
3	The department is receptive to new ideas		
4	Individual student records are detailed and frequently updated		
5	Schemes of work give detailed and clear guidance		
6	Opportunities are made for career development through appropriate delegation		
7	The department shows selectivity when considering innovations		
8	The department keeps abreast of recent developments in the teaching of the subject		
9	Marking is consistent and adheres to clear criteria		
10	The content of schemes of work is periodically reviewed		
11	Designated roles in the department play to the strengths of individuals		
12	Resources are well deployed and targeted on priorities		
13	Students are aware of the marking criteria for assessments		
14	The schemes of work detail a range of teaching and learning styles		
15	The department is united in its attitude towards all key policies		
16	Resources are well organized and arranged		
17	Teachers are involved in making decisions on key issues		
18	The department has a sense of 'group spirit'		
19	There is an effective procedure for student self-assessment		
20	Student records are used effectively to monitor the progress of individual students		
21	Effective use is made of in-class support for special needs		
22	Teachers in the department support each other		
23	Examination results are analysed thoroughly to assist in raising achievement		
24	Able students are stretched and challenged		
25	Interpersonal relationships in the department contribute to effective team work		
26	Students are well prepared for external exams		
27	You feel able to raise issues that you feel strongly about		
28	The department has a clear sense of where it is going		
29	There are systematic procedures for the moderation of assessments		
30	Departmental meetings feature developmental as well as administrative tasks		
31	Opportunities are created for colleagues to share good practice		
32	Effective support is provided in the department when behaviour problems occur		
33	Clear priorities for development are identified and adhered to		
34	Student achievement is celebrated		
35	Day-to-day routine tasks are efficiently organized		
36	The department integrates with the main body of teaching staff		
37	Staff achievement is celebrated		
38	Student achievement is rewarded		
39	Students' work is well displayed		
40	The work of the department is effectively promoted		

Table 9.2   Departmental survey

Development planning is a cyclical process involving audit, construction, implementation and evaluation. It involves planning for the maintenance of aspects of provision which are effective as well as planning to develop areas of weakness. It is important that planned developments are realistic and achievable, that people know clearly who is responsible, that clear time-scales are agreed and that success criteria are established at the planning stage.

Collaboration, openness and critical reflection are essential when teams are evaluating their performance. Collective ownership of the development plan with key tasks shared between team members is important for effective implementation. Team leaders need regularly to review progress so as to avoid developments falling behind agreed schedules.

CHAPTER TEN

Evaluating Performance

Introduction

When it comes to the formal evaluation of the performance of colleagues, many middle managers seem to get cold feet, despite making informal judgements about members of their team day in and day out. Evaluating performance of self and others is, in fact, a key aspect of middle management. In future, the most successful individuals and schools are likely to be those who are the most effective learners. In a supportive culture individuals should be able to see that, ultimately, the pupils gain from the evaluation of teachers, because the purpose of the exercise is to improve teaching and thus pupil performance. With a national agenda for improving performance in schools some politicians would like to see appraisal formally linked to teachers' pay and promotion. This chapter, however, will concentrate on 'using the process to develop the personal and professional effectiveness of the appraisee' (TTA 1998), a function listed in *National Standards for Subject Leaders*.

Much has already been made in this book of the importance of getting the culture right. In promoting a collaborative team culture you will be helping to create the conditions for improvement and fostering commitment to continuous learning and development. These are essential preconditions for valid monitoring and evaluation. While the governing body and head teacher have ultimate responsibility for this it is likely that it will be partly delegated to team leaders, though the extent to which a subject leader or pastoral team leader is involved in monitoring will depend on school policy.

Monitoring, evaluation and review

Monitoring, evaluation and review are separate processes, though they are usually linked. Monitoring is concerned with the systematic collection of data to establish how well, say, a subject team is performing.

Monitoring provides the evidence for evaluation, which is concerned with issues of quality; it involves considering whether or not performance or service could be improved. The review process is concerned with using the outcomes from monitoring and evaluation to develop strategies for improving performance or service. Many teachers associate monitoring and evaluation with accountability but a more powerful reason for engaging in monitoring and evaluation is that it helps a team or school to consider how things might be done better in the future. In other words, the process can benefit children. In effective schools, monitoring, evaluation and review are integral elements of the school development planning process (see Chapter 9).

The prospect of monitoring provision and standards may seem overwhelming to a newly appointed middle manager. It is important, therefore, to break the task down into manageable parts. There are several important sources of evidence which can be used: documents relating to curriculum planning; qualitative feedback on the experienced curriculum; observation of teaching; and quantitative statistical data relating to pupil performance.

An audit of planning undertaken collectively can be a good starting point. It can provide an effective opportunity for colleagues to identify areas for departmental development and improvement. A collaborative approach to auditing curriculum plans can be an effective staff development exercise. The implication that colleagues are being monitored can be avoided in favour of sharing good practice and agreeing goals and classroom strategies. Asking teachers to submit their weekly lesson plans for 'inspection' is much less common in secondary schools than primary and it would be counter-productive for a head of department to try and introduce such a system if it was not already common practice. However, if a team leader had clear evidence that a colleague was seriously under-performing then looking at their lesson planning may be an important aspect of the support needed to bring about improvement. Likewise, NQTs are entitled to support from their team leader, who will probably be their designated induction tutor. One way in which this can be done is through regular discussions which focus on lesson plans.

Evidence for monitoring the experienced curriculum can come from colleagues, pupils and parents. Discussions with team members can yield useful information about children's responses to particular approaches, activities and resources and pupils can certainly provide useful feedback through course review questionnaires. Parents will often comment at consultation evenings on whether or not their child has enjoyed a particular subject. Of course, team leaders must use evidence gained from all sources with caution: a small number of dissatisfied pupils does not mean a course has been badly taught, for example. More systematic monitoring and evaluation can be achieved through moderation exercises. The benefits of discussing individual pieces of work are considerable. It is likely that at GCSE level moderation will be an exam board requirement, but it is also good practice to develop this in years 7–9 with pieces of work for portfolios used to assist in assessing pupils in relation to national curriculum levels. Try and develop a culture in which colleagues in your team are used to looking together at work produced by pupils they teach. Collecting and analysing such samples can assist in focusing discussion on expectations and standards. *Learning schools* are not frightened of discovering what has worked well and what not so well. Armed with this information they can plan for improvement.

In some schools team leaders engage in direct classroom observation. Where this is imposed as a result of an SMT decree it is unlikely to be very productive. However, if staff accept the legitimacy of the process and see the likelihood of real gains for their pupils then focused observation may be very useful. The emphasis must be on observation as a means of supporting improvement in performance rather than as a method for making negative judgements about colleagues. Certainly, there is much to be gained from teachers watching excellent practitioners at work as teaching has an element of performance art about it. Skilful practitioners may also be able to offer tips and advice to colleagues they observe. Often, teachers seem very willing to do this for student teachers and NQTs but are more embarrassed when it comes to sharing good practice with more experienced colleagues.

The criteria used by OFSTED inspectors for judging the quality of teaching can provide a useful framework for observation and discussion. The Inspection Schedule requires inspectors to base their judgements on the extent to which teachers:

- have a secure knowledge and understanding of the subject they teach;
- set high expectations to challenge pupils and add to their knowledge and understanding;
- plan effectively;
- use methods which match lesson objectives and the needs of all pupils;
- manage pupils well and achieve effective discipline;
- use time and resources effectively;
- assess pupils' work and use assessment to inform planning.

Seeing lesson observation as part of an on-going strategy for raising standards will only be possible if a school has developed an ethos in which colleagues are committed to continuous improvement through collaboration. Team leaders must be willing to be observed by colleagues, both to demonstrate good practice and to gain feedback concerning specific aspects of their own practice, as well as being observers.

Using pupil performance data

There is a considerable amount of quantitative data available to assist the head of department in evaluating the performance of their area. The results of internally devised tests and exams, SATs results, GCSE results and A-level results are all useful. However, the important thing is to avoid making comparisons between colleagues on raw data alone or on very limited samples. For example, a number of tests may be used by a department with all Year 7 pupils. Comparing the results in these tests of one teacher's class with another will only be meaningful if you are certain that all groups contain pupils of similar ability and that these pupils all began Year 7 with a similar level of knowledge and understanding. Even in mixed ability groups it does not follow that all groups really do contain a normal distribution of all abilities, therefore judgements based on raw test scores would be flawed.

For this reason a reliable baseline test is required and it is a good idea for teams to write such a test for their subject. Once a Year 7 pupil has a baseline test score it is possible to compare their subsequent test scores with pupils who had the same baseline test scores. In this way a 'value-added' figure can be arrived at. This is a better way of comparing the performance of one teacher's pupils with another, though it is still very dangerous to jump to conclusions on the basis of small numbers of pupils. The use of such data to identify particular pupils who appear to be under-performing in order to target them for support would, of course, be good practice. Learning schools ensure that teams analyse value-added data together in order to look for trends and evidence of good practice boosting results. If one teacher, for example, seemed to be successful in helping the very able to make exceptional progress then their methods would be worth sharing with other colleagues.

This approach still has its limitations. Even when there is clear evidence of value added it is not clear whether you are adding greater value than other schools dealing with pupils of similar ability. This is where evidence from sources such as Durham University's value-added information system, headed by Professor Carol Fitz-Gibbon, becomes useful. Around a quarter of secondary schools in England currently use ALIS (A-level information system) and YELLIS (Year 11 information system) in order to establish how well students in their school are performing compared with *similar students* nationally.

In the case of YELLIS all students complete two tests (mathematics and vocabulary) and a questionnaire on their 'cultural capital' in Year 10. The results are processed to place students into one of four bands A to D. 'Chances graphs' are provided to give indicators of potential student performance within these bands in a wide range of GCSE subjects. These are derived from a large-scale sample of past performance. After a school's GCSE results have been analysed, the school receives feedback on the performance of each department within the school measured against each other, to give a positive or negative 'residual'. The GCSE performance of students by subject is also compared with similar students in other schools to produce residuals for each department. This can be seen as the 'value-added' measure of each department in the school. By looking at the results for each student, it is possible to see how students taught by member of staff X have performed compared with students taught by member of staff Y.

The important difference between this data and raw performance data is that it comes much closer to comparing like with like. With this information it is not possible for a colleague to explain away poor pupil performance with excuses like 'my group was weaker', 'children always do less well in this particular subject because it is harder' or 'the results are good for the children in our school'. Clearly, small numbers of pupils will still limit the validity of conclusions reached from the data but there is no doubt that the ALIS/YELLIS information helps a head of department to ask the right questions about the achievement of pupils taught by teachers in their team. Used sensitively, the data can help colleagues in a team become more reflective and analytical and can help to pinpoint areas of excellent performance as well as areas of concern. Where excellent value added is in evidence praising the teacher concerned and sharing the good practice that produced the results are essential.

Appraisal and target setting

Appraisal procedures in any school depend on the organizational climate and culture and middle managers will have to operate within existing arrangements. Appraisal has had a somewhat chequered history. In some schools appraisal has been almost completely ignored while in others it has become an accepted feature of the organization. The benefits of effective appraisal include improved inter-personal relationships, reciprocal learning through observation and discussion, improved self-esteem through positive feedback and access to appropriate training, if required. However, the experience in many schools is that appraisal has been under-resourced in terms of both time and access to training and that it has lacked any hard edge, thus the impact on pupil achievement resulting from appraisal of teaching has not been measurable. It is likely that appraisal will become very much more important if the proposals outlined in the 1998 government green paper are followed through. These proposals include a new layer of professional teachers who have achieved *threshold performance* and thus access to a higher salary. One feature of the new system would be 'new appraisal arrangements involving a thorough annual assessment of teachers' performance against agreed objectives' (DfEE 1988).

If appraisal in future becomes linked to teachers' pay then it could pose a real threat to the team ethos and culture which has been encouraged in this book. People are much less likely to want to share good practice if their salary levels depend on them demonstrating a higher level of skill than their colleagues. Likewise, observation of classroom performance takes on a different feel if it is associated with determining pay levels rather than encouraging colleagues to identify areas of weakness in order to be given the necessary support to improve. For these reasons it is advisable to keep staff development appraisal and performance appraisal separate. However, all appraisal programmes are heavy on staff time and this needs to be born in mind when decisions on approaches are being made.

In using appraisal to help staff development target setting will be necessary. A target is a particular aspect of work agreed by appraiser and teacher to be raised to a high priority for achievement within a set time scale. A target may be:

- part of a basic task in which there is unacceptable performance (e.g. regular failure to meet agreed administrative deadlines);
- an aspect of classroom performance (e.g. improving differentiation);
- a delegated responsibility (e.g. to complete the annual textbook order);
- a specifically nominated project (e.g. to write a new scheme of work);
- a personal one related to the teacher's professional development (e.g. chairing departmental meetings).

In a well-managed appraisal interview it is quite likely that the teacher will propose targets for improvement. In a few cases it may be necessary for the appraiser to do so. Good team relationships and a vision of continuous improvement will, of course, help to make target setting both natural and uncontroversial.

Dealing with incompetent teachers

Subject leaders and pastoral team leaders are increasingly being made accountable for under-performance in their team. With the current emphasis on target setting and the wealth of statistical information now available on pupil achievement this trend is likely to increase. Middle managers must, therefore, establish the nature of the under-performance and devise strategies to raise standards and develop the skills of under-performing team members. Fortunately, inspection evidence shows that most teachers are competent or better and there is advice provided in Chapter 4 on how to get the best out of such colleagues. In the case of teachers faced with incompetence allegations the Teaching Competence Project, directed by Ted Wragg at the University of Exeter, found that about a quarter of them were able to improve their performance. Effective support and the teachers' desire to improve were key factors in these successes.

When judging a teacher's competence it is important not to act purely on first impressions, anecdotes or information provided by others. There are many different styles of teaching and you should not jump to conclusions about a teacher's competence simply because their style of teaching is idiosyncratic. If there is clear evidence of under-performance based on a significant amount of pupil achievement data or if repeated negative comments about a teacher are being made then you need to investigate. Evidence needs to be gathered from a variety of sources including observation of lessons, inspection of students' work, lesson plans, pupil course evaluations and pupil performance data. In well-managed teams these forms of evidence will be being regularly discussed and any under-achievement is likely to be out in the open anyway.

If you feel that there is indeed under-performance, your initial strategy must be one of support. Try coaching first, but if there is no improvement then the colleague must be informed of your concerns. These must be clearly expressed and you must try and temper specific criticism with praise for what is going well, wherever possible. The initial interview should be minuted and should provide opportunities for the under-performer to respond and provide an explanation or express a viewpoint. Targets should be set, with a time limit for their achievement and a date for review. These should be realistic and challenging and the time-scale manageable, generally within a term.

Under-performance in the classroom can result from teachers simply becoming complacent or may be because they failed to develop basic classroom management strategies during their early years of teaching. It is very rare for teachers to be incompetent in all aspects of their work and context can be very important. Teachers sometimes cope well with some groups but not others; successful teachers in some schools may flounder when they move to a school with a very different intake of pupils. Assistance must be offered to enable under-performers to improve. Some additional training may be necessary and it might be appropriate for another colleague to assume a mentoring role rather than you. In some circumstances, under-performance may be caused by factors outside school such as the break-up of a marriage. Such situations may be temporary and, with your support, the problem can soon be resolved. However, it is important to put the needs of the students first. Personal problems may be a reason for under-performance but not a justification. Sympathy and support are vital but if you and senior colleagues allow very poor performance to continue for several terms or even years you are failing in your duty as managers. According to Maureen Cooper, writing for governors:

Sometimes the downward slide has gone on for some time before any formal efforts have been made by management to improve the situation. You could say that in this situation you've got two failures to deal with: not only the under-performing teacher but also the failure of management to deal with the problem early enough. (*TES*, 9 October 1998)

Senior managers must be kept informed of the targets you have agreed and if these targets are not met a review meeting must move matters forward. Discuss the implications of the meeting with the appropriate senior member of staff. If you have supported and praised while at the same time being clear about the areas that need to be improved you have acted reasonably. There is no 'quick-fix' for under-performing teachers and in the end it may be that disciplinary procedures have to be initiated. This will be the responsibility of senior members of staff but it is important that you have done all you can to help your colleague improve before this point. If disciplinary proceedings are started you will, of course, be involved and you need to seek advice from your union. You will need to keep detailed records of all meetings and targets. Disciplinary proceedings can be stressful both for the colleague concerned and their team leader. Whatever the justice of your case it is likely that the teacher concerned will feel defensive and betrayed. The ethos of the team will almost certainly be affected. You must, therefore, be certain that a member of staff is under-performing and that this under-performance is detrimental to the pupils and to your team before proceedings commence.

Summary

Middle managers should be prepared to embrace the idea of formally evaluating the performance of colleagues and they must work hard to create the kind of open and supportive culture which makes appraisal a natural and unthreatening feature of departmental organization. Spreading good practice and enabling colleagues to improve aspects of their work are necessary if pupil performance is to be improved.

There is now a wealth of data available relating to the performance of pupils. The use of this data is important for evaluating a department's performance, development planning and setting future targets and it may also be helpful in appraising individual teachers, if used with caution.

While there are very few incompetent teachers if a middle manager has evidence that a colleague is seriously under-performing then it is important to grasp the nettle by putting in place a programme of support and targets to help the member of staff to improve. In extreme circumstances it may be necessary to consider disciplinary procedures or dismissal. This will be a matter for senior managers to handle but it is vital that you work closely with them, adhere to procedures and keep accurate records of all meetings with the colleague concerned.

CHAPTER ELEVEN

Stress Management and Time Management

Introduction

It is important in a book on middle management to consider the management of stress as the pressures and demands on middle managers are such that some potential for stress almost inevitably goes with the territory. Of course, school middle managers and indeed teachers are not the only people who have to deal with stress; many would argue that stress is endemic to modern working life and that understanding the causes of stress and strategies for dealing with it are therefore essential life-skills. Managers certainly have a responsibility to be aware of when they are stressed themselves and of when those they manage are stressed. In their approach to team relationships managers can greatly reduce the stress felt by others and by managing their own stress appropriately they can make themselves more efficient, more effective and more self-fulfilled.

Many people feel that lack of time to do jobs properly is a major cause of stress and because of the perceived link between time and stress time management is also considered in this chapter. Being able to organize time effectively is essential for all managers; those who are unable to do this will find that work encroaches further and further into their evenings, weekends and holidays and, except in the case of workaholics, this in itself will become a major source of stress. The good news is that there are some surprisingly simple techniques for improving time management and, while some people seem to be *naturally* better at managing time than others, everyone can improve their time management if they are determined to do so.

Some thoughts on stress

According to the Education Service Advisory Committee (1992) stress at work is 'a process that can occur when there is a mismatch between the perceived pressures of the work situation and the individual's ability to cope with it'. David Fontana (1989) defined stress as

a demand made upon the adaptive capacities of the mind and body. If these capacities can handle the demand and enjoy the stimulation involved, then stress is welcome and helpful. If they can't and find the demand debilitating, then stress is unwelcome and unhelpful.

This definition is useful for several reasons. First, it reminds us that stress can be both good and bad. Secondly, it isn't so much pressure that determine whether we're stressed or not, it is our reactions to it. Thirdly, if our body's capacities are good enough, we respond well to stress, if they aren't we give way. Typically, too little pressure results in boredom and frustration, a moderate level of pressure is stimulating and actually improves performance whereas too much pressure becomes debilitating and reduces performance (Figure 11.1).

Each individual, of course, has a different capacity for dealing with pressure and so a task that causes little anxiety for one person may cause considerable anxiety for another. Much depends on the individual's personality, experience and motivation, as well as support received from colleagues and managers, as to how they will react to a potentially stressful situation. In addition the experiences that people are encountering outside the workplace are important. A stressful domestic situation coupled with pressure in the workplace could produce an intolerable level of stress for some people. It is very important, therefore, that managers encourage a

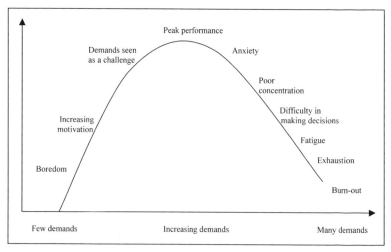

Figure 11.1   The effect of increasing pressure on performance at work

collaborative and open culture in which colleagues are willing to talk about stressful situations they face and in which people support each other. An effective manager should be able to gauge the level of pressure needed for the most effective performance of each team member. A newly qualified teacher may be finding the behaviour of a particular class stressful whereas an experienced colleague may be undergoing the stress of marital separation, which is having an impact on their working life. Clearly, there are ways in which an effective manager could provide support in order to help both colleagues. This would be likely to generate respect and appreciation and to be repaid with goodwill in the future.

Causes of stress

It is generally acknowledged that death of a spouse, divorce, marital separation, death of a close family member and pregnancy are all causes of stress. These events are clearly outside the control of middle managers, though being aware of them happening in the lives of team members and responding with sensitivity is important. Across a wide range of jobs the following are regularly mentioned as causes of stress: nature of supervision, relationships with supervisor, relationships with peers, working conditions, salary, status and job insecurity. Some of these are outside the control of middle managers in schools but some can be very much affected by them. Relationships feature very strongly as causes of stress which underlines the importance of creating the positive relationships and empowering culture advocated throughout this book.

I regularly conduct surveys of the causes of stress in teaching with my management classes. While not claiming any reliability for the results it is interesting that the same causes are always listed. These include:
- heavy workload;
- constant change;
- not enough time to do things thoroughly;
- OFSTED inspections;
- being unable to satisfy the conflicting and increasing demands of parents, pupils and managers;
- negative media coverage of education;
- lack of respect from society;
- lack of recognition for skills;
- increasing accountability but decreasing professional freedom;
- not knowing how colleagues rate you;
- not feeling valued for all the time devoted to the job.

According to Gold and Evans (1998) 'an unresolved mismatch between a personal philosophy of education and the organization's educational philosophy' is also a potential source of stress. This, and many of the points made above, can be directly influenced by middle managers. Productive relationships and a collaborative team culture are essential for minimizing stress. Recognizing skills, increasing autonomy, involvement in decision-making, providing effective feedback on performance and praising commitment are all things that have been encouraged in this book. Middle managers can also influence workload, how change is managed and response to OFSTED inspections.

According to the National Association of Head Teachers, increased illness among teachers who go through OFSTED inspection is not uncommon. In a survey of 1,220 heads, 40 per cent said staff illness increased in the three months following inspection. One possible explanation for this, provided by Elaine Williams (*TES*, 26 March 1999), is that teachers are unable to separate work and personal identity. Teaching is so personal that when OFSTED comes into a school they feel *they* are being assessed not their teaching. If they are criticized they can begin to feel worthless as *individuals*. Likewise, if they are praised their self-esteem is boosted and they feel good about *themselves*, not just their teaching.

Good middle managers help to minimize the stress of an inspection by ensuring that their house is in order and there is therefore nothing to be anxious about. Good teams have a positive ethos, clear goals, well-designed schemes of work, good monitoring procedures and effective teaching. With these things in place there is little to fear from inspection. Confident middle managers are proud of their team's achievements and will want to help inspectors to see their area at its best by being proactive from the start. If middle managers have confidence in their team and are relaxed about inspection because they know all is well they will be helping team members to feel confident and in control. Of course, if a department is not effective, if confidence is unjustified because all is not well or if there is a panic leading up to inspection to put things right it will not be easy for team members to feel in control and confident. In these circumstances stress is much more likely and the ineffective middle manager must accept a major part of the responsibility for this.

Identifying stress

Someone suffering stress may exhibit some or all of the following symptoms:
- a general deterioration in performance at work;
- an increase in sickness absence, which may fall into a particular pattern of frequent short periods of absence, possibly due to stress

symptoms such as headaches, difficulty breathing, poor sleep patterns, indigestion and palpitations;

- an increase in irritability resulting in conflict and tension with other colleagues and a deterioration in relationships;
- loss of motivation and job satisfaction;
- less contact with people outside work;
- in some cases, overeating and/or an increase in alcohol consumption.

If stress is not tackled it can result in high blood pressure, heart disease, anxiety, depression, ulcers and thyroid disorders.

Controlling the stress of team members

The responsibility for the creation of a safe place of work lies with the employer but it is down to senior and middle managers to enact this responsibility. Sound management can prevent teachers and other employees becoming over-stressed in several ways.

- The school and team culture should ensure that stress is not seen as a weakness in the individual and that employees suffering stress will receive support without being made to feel guilty.
- The job itself must be manageable and the person's abilities, skills and experience must match the requirements for the job.
- Stress often occurs during periods of change. Team involvement in planning and managing change will go a long way towards reducing its negative impacts.
- Training must be provided to assist teachers in meeting the demands of change.
- Effective communication must exist so teachers have an accurate perception of the role they have to perform.

These points, of course, need also to be considered by senior managers in relation to their handling of middle managers.

Controlling your own stress

Psychologists identify some individuals as being more stress prone than others. They are usually people who have high expectations of themselves, are very task- and result-orientated, tend to work very quickly and find inefficiency in others very frustrating. It is, of course, much harder for such people to control stress than other personality types, but not impossible. Recognizing your potential for stress and being proactive in controlling stress are both very important. If stress really is endemic to modern working environments then it is important to anticipate it and develop strategies that will prevent you becoming stressed rather than waiting until you feel stressed and then considering what you ought to do about it. Here are a few pointers on reducing stress:

- *Get your time management right* (see below). This will make you much more effective in all aspects of your job.
- *Maintain a sense of humour.* Take what you do seriously but don't take yourself too seriously. It is important in teaching to be able to laugh at yourself and if you cultivate humour as part of the team culture this will be a real antidote to the pressure of the job.
- *Remain optimistic.* If you focus on the negative you will soon get yourself on a downward spiral. It is very important to think positive, and recognize the progress made rather than dwelling on the distance still to go. Hackneyed as the phrase may be it really is important to see your glass as half full rather than half empty.
- *Have a life beyond work.* It is essential that you engage in activities away from school. A successful family life and satisfying social life make you a more interesting and rounded person. Too many late nights at the word processor or too many working weekends build tension and resentment. It is in everybody's best interests that you remain healthy and positive and knowing when to 'draw the line' with work is important. Of course, there will be some evenings and weekends when it is simply impossible to avoid school work but an effective manager does not need to be on the job twenty-four hours a day.
- *Establish clear boundaries between work and home.* Some managers arrive at school an hour before the school day begins and work on until 5.00 or 5.30 p.m. and then take no work home. While this wouldn't suit everybody (flexibility over non-contact tasks can help greatly with child minding arrangements, for example) it is one way of clearly demarcating working life and home life which really can help you to 'switch off' once you leave the school buildings.
- *Learn not to take things personally.* Managers must be able to cope with healthy debate and argument and not be distressed if things do not always go according to plan. A good team is one that allows discussion and diversity of views and managers need not feel threatened by this.
- *Exercise.* Obviously, your age will determine the kind of exercise that you can perform but it is important to engage in some form of regular exercise as a means of reducing stress through the release of endorphins.
- *Avoid getting in a rut.* Taking up a new post can be stressful but it is also true that for some people staying in one job for too long can become a cause of stress. With a new job there is much excitement

and challenge; you are trying to prove yourself and often don't notice or resent the hours you are putting in due to the satisfaction derived from the impact you are making. Once you have been in post a few years devoting long hours to what have become routine tasks rather than challenges can become a source of irritation. If this is the way you feel then it might be time to think about a job move; motivating others becomes very difficult if you are no longer motivated yourself.

Some thoughts on time management

The principles and skills of time management are just as relevant to teachers and managers in education as they are to managers in other walks of life. In an ever more demanding and stressful profession effective time management is vital for survival. Far too many middle managers find themselves *living to work* rather than *working to live*; a situation that is simply not sustainable in the long run and which can cause burn-out and serious health problems. Many teachers devote very long hours to their work out of genuine commitment and a desire to do the best for the children they teach. While this is admirable in one sense *expecting* teachers to devote every evening and weekend to their jobs in order to maintain the nation's education system is simply not acceptable and is actually a recipe for stress-related illnesses and marriage breakdowns among teachers.

Effective teachers and managers learn to use time efficiently. It is very revealing to discover that those complaining the most in staff rooms about lack of time are often very inefficient in their use of time. Likewise, teachers who are actively involved in extra-curricular activities and award bearing INSET are often also the very members of staff who can be relied upon to get a job done efficiently. Indeed, it is very likely that they also have fulfilling family lives and an active social life. Some people seem to be *naturally* good time managers and this is reflected in all areas of their lives. Even so, there are strategies which everybody can use to become better time managers.

How is effective time management achieved?

There is a difference between doing a job effectively and doing a job efficiently. Effectiveness means doing a job to the required standard whereas efficiency involves doing it in the right way and at the right time. Good time management helps people to increase their efficiency and maintain or improve their effectiveness. In recent years teachers have had to cope with increases in workload and the only certainty about the future is that change in education will continue as more and more is expected of our schools. Being effective and efficient in such a climate is essential. Working smarter not harder is the way to survive and this requires a systematic approach to work and to life in general.

According to Iain D. Wood (1991) there are three characteristics of effective time managers which he calls the 'three Ts':

- **Thought**   They achieve their goals by thinking about what they have to do, questioning its value and prioritizing.
- **Technique**   They plan when and how they will undertake each task so as to optimize their use of time.
- **Temperament**   They try not to panic when new tasks come along because they realize that worrying wastes time and solves nothing. Likewise, when things go wrong they do not spend hours thinking 'if only I had …'. Instead, they conduct a review of why things went wrong and then plan to ensure that the same mistakes are not made in the future.

Planning, prioritizing and deadlines

There is a cliché that suggests that if we fail to plan then we plan to fail. All effective middle managers need to plan so that they can spread their workload and prioritize. Making effective use of a planner/diary is essential and some practical tips on this are provided in Chapter 8 in the section on 'Administration'.

Covey (1994) suggests a variation on planning by use of a time-management matrix (Table 11.1). All tasks should fit into one of these categories. Obviously, the urgent and important matters require your immediate attention. Items in the other boxes must be dealt with in order of priority. At the bottom of the scale non-urgent and unimportant tasks should probably be crossed off your list all together. It is useful to try and predict the amount of time needed for each activity beforehand. Bear in mind, though, that initially it is likely that you will underestimate the time required than overestimate it. With practice you will become more accurate, and the knowledge gained will prove invaluable for future planning.

Setting deadlines for the activities on your list is a good way of focusing the mind and avoiding 'drift' which results in important but not urgent tasks never being tackled. Deadlines for all tasks must be realistic and you should avoid setting deadlines that result in you putting off tasks until the day before they have to be completed. 'Working to the wire' is a bad habit and one that you should plan to avoid. It allows no further time to reschedule the work should a crisis arise. Set your own target date for

	Urgent	Not urgent
Important	• Crises • Pressing problems • Dead-line driven projects, meetings	• Preparation • Prevention • Planning • Values clarification • Relationship building • Empowerment

Not important	• Interruptions, some
	  phone calls
	• Some mail, some
	  reports
	• Some meetings
	• Many pressing
	  matters
	• Many popular
	  activities
		• Trivia
		• Junk mail
		• Some phone calls
		• Time wasters
		• 'Escape' activities

Table 11.1 Covey's time management matrix

completing each task some time in advance of the school deadline. This provides a safety net should a crisis arise. Encourage this practice in your team by negotiating deadlines for work you need from them which gives some flexibility in case of illness or absence. Encourage a total quality management approach so team members see one another and see you as 'internal clients'. If deadlines are missed then someone is being let down and put under pressure, which is not fair. A supportive and empowering team ethos does not mean being sloppy about deadlines. If these are negotiated then everyone should adhere to them.

Delegation

If management is the art of getting things done through people then delegation is essential to good management. Most middle managers spend time doing things which should or could be done by someone else. Delegation should not be abdication but, used properly, should be a feature of effective team work and staff development. As we saw in Chapter 4 delegating needs to be used in conjunction with supporting, coaching and directing in order to get the best out of team members. In Chapter 5 we considered an effective team to be one that used the strengths of each team player by delegating tasks appropriately. Where there is a gap between the current ability of a person to carry out a task and their potential ability, it is well worth spending time instructing them. Staff training is a good investment in the future, when team members will be able to complete tasks with decreasing levels of supervision. It can be tempting to try to do everything yourself, because it seems quicker, for fear of being outshone by a colleague or simply because you feel you are paid to do more. However, fair and effective delegation is a must for middle managers and should be cultivated as a key feature of supportive teamwork.

Making decisions and being assertive

Procrastination can be a great time waster. While it is a mistake to make snap decisions before you have all the necessary information, dithering between choice A and choice B will not make the eventual judgement any more correct. Managers must be able to weigh up the facts and make decisions, even if they don't always get them right! Another form of procrastination is continually putting off jobs you don't like doing. Competent time managers identify the tasks they least like doing and use strategies to help them overcome their natural reticence to do them. Strategies include:
- setting deadlines for completion of unpopular tasks;
- breaking tasks down into manageable stages;
- tackling difficult jobs early in the day when they are fresh;
- rewarding themselves for finishing a task;
- getting a colleague to check that they have done the work.

When it comes to paperwork procrastination must be avoided. There are three options with paperwork: deal with it straight away; deal with it later; or put it in the bin. It is essential that junk mail is put straight in the bin. Correspondence and memos that can be dealt with quickly should be attended to on the day they arrive in your pigeonhole. Paperwork that will require more serious attention should be listed in your planner as a job to be dealt with. Try not to let paper pile up on your desk. Use your filing system to save you time. Make good use of technology also. Handbooks, class lists, letters to parents, exam papers, schemes of work, worksheets etc. should all be stored on disc so that they can be modified easily rather than completely rewritten.

Assertiveness is another essential ingredient in good time management. There are occasions when even the most caring manager needs to complete an urgent and important task and so does not want interrupting. If you are respected by colleagues and provide support and encouragement, setting aside some time when you don't want interrupting should not be seen as unreasonable. Likewise, if one of your team is in the middle of an urgent task then you should not expect them to drop everything in order to discuss some less important matter with you.

Sometimes middle managers feel under pressure because of tasks with unrealistic deadlines set by senior colleagues. It is very important for middle managers *as a group* to be strong if they are presented with unreasonable requests from senior managers. When asked individually to undertake a task it is difficult to say no because you don't want to offend senior colleagues or appear uncooperative or lazy. However, by taking on too many new tasks aspects of your existing work might begin to suffer and so it is important to learn how to say no without offending. The art of saying no diplomatically lies not so much in what you say but in the way you say it. Speak with confidence, be honest and say what you feel in a controlled way. Try not to allow your emotions to be demonstrated. Do not be sarcastic or aggressive. Don't apologise profusely or put yourself down. Sometimes a compromise rather than a refusal is possible.

Some suggestions of how to say no tactfully include:

- I feel honoured that you have asked me but ...
- Yes, but it will have to wait until after ...
- Yes, but I couldn't finish it by ... because I have ... to do.
- I would be happy to do that but let me know which you would like me to do first as I already have ... to do.
- It would be possible but if I devote time to ... I won't be able to do ... so which would you prefer?

Effective time management does not mean saying no to everything, it is just one of many strategies not a quick-fix solution to your workload. Indeed, if used to excess there is a danger that others will see you as uncooperative. A collegiate 'can do' culture cannot be created by people who say no to everything but, equally, hardworking and competent managers and teachers should not feel guilty if they occasionally say no, especially to requests likely to impact negatively on existing areas of their work.

Self-assessment and reflection

Are you a stress-prone person?

Below are a series of questions to help you identify how stress-prone you or your colleagues are. They are based on a questionnaire provided by Cooper and Sutherland (1997). Give yourself or your colleague a score on a 1–11 scale for the bi-polar statements provided. The first one has the scale included so you can see where low and high scores fall.

Casual about appointments   1 2 3 4 5 6 7 8 9 10 11   Never late
Not competitive – Very competetive

Good listener – Anticipates what others are going to say (attempts to finish for them)

Never feels rushed, even when under pressure – Always rushed

Can wait patiently – Impatient while waiting

Takes things one at a time – Tries to do many things at once

Slow, deliberate talker – Fast and forceful speaker

Cares about satisfying him/herself no matter what others may think – Wants a good job recognized by others

Slow doing things – Fast at doing things (eating, walking etc.)

Easy-going – Hard-driving, pushing yourself and others

Expresses feelings – Hides feelings

Many outside interests – Few interests outside work/home

Unambitious – Ambitious

Casual – Eager to get things done

Reflection

The higher the score received on this questionnaire, the more firmly an individual can be classed as stress-prone. People who are highly stress-prone are, in fact, often blind to their own behaviour. If you are scoring this questionnaire to assess your own personality and suspect that you are stress-prone it is likely that you will find it hard to be completely honest in your self-assessment. To get a more accurate assessment it is useful to ask someone else who knows you well to complete the questionnaire based on their perceptions of your workplace behaviour.

Psychologists use the term 'Type A personality' for those who exhibit strong stress-prone tendencies. Such people can actually be very difficult to work with. They display the following characteristics:

- devotion to work, working long hours, feeling guilty when not working;
- a chronic sense of time urgency;
- attempting to schedule more and more into less and less time;
- often attempting to do two or more things at the same time;
- hate being kept waiting, especially in queues;
- find it difficult to talk about anything other than work;
- a strong need to be in control;
- a very competitive outlook.

The reason why Type A people can be difficult to work with is because of their constant need to compete. They tend not to be good listeners and like to keep strict control over what is going on. They often do jobs themselves rather than taking the time to show someone else what to do, so they fail to develop their staff and rarely delegate. They often expect everyone around them to work to their demanding pace and schedule, including long hours of working and skipping lunch breaks in order to meet unrealistic goals and deadlines. Ironically, Type A people are often rewarded with promotion because, in the short term at least, they manage to move things forward. In the longer term, however, Type A behaviour becomes dysfunctional for an organization.

It is important that managers who recognize Type A behaviour in themselves consider what effect they might have on others in their team. Arguably, it is impossible to change personality but it is possible to modify some behaviour associated with personality. Reflective managers with Type A tendencies, therefore, must be aware of the potential dysfunctional effects of their competitiveness and drive and must acknowledge that their desire to control will not help to produce an effective and empowered team. Through knowledge comes strength and with greater self-awareness Type A middle managers can adapt their behaviour so that they maintain their sense of drive but use management techniques that are likely to produce effective and focused teams. The techniques required for this have been stressed throughout this book.

Summary

Too little pressure can result in boredom, a moderate level of pressure is stimulating but too much pressure causes stress and thus reduces performance. An effective middle manager should know his or her team well and be able to judge the level of pressure needed to get the best performance out of each team member. They will protect their team from unnecessary stress by encouraging a supportive and open culture and manage their own stress by cultivating a positive outlook and ensuring that they have a fulfilling life beyond school.

Stress management and time management are linked. By using time efficiently middle managers can increase their effectiveness and reduce stress. Considering what constitutes inefficient use of time and the thinking that goes with it can help to clarify the strategies that can be used to improve time management. Consider the following and then do the opposite:

- Don't invest in a planner and never have your diary to hand – you have a good memory and that should be enough.
- Don't bother with targets – team members might feel too pressured.
- Never prioritize the tasks you have to do – you work more efficiently when you suddenly realize the deadline is tomorrow.
- Don't make a daily list of things to do – if a task is really necessary someone will remind you it needs doing.

- Never delegate – you're paid to do more and team members have enough on with teaching.
- Never say no, however unreasonable the request – senior management might think you lack commitment.
- Never reply to memos immediately – decisions are always better for being given plenty of thought.
- Allow people to interrupt you at all times – it shows you are a caring manager.
- Never throw junk mail straight in the bin – you need to consider whether it might come in handy one day.
- Each day and at weekends take as much paperwork home as you can manage to transfer from your desk to your briefcase – the more you have with you the more you are likely to do.
- Don't store class lists, letters to parents, schemes of work, handbooks, worksheets, exam papers etc. on a word processor – you rewrite them every year anyway so what's the point?

Links to TTA Priorities for Middle Managers

Throughout this book reference has been made to *National Standards for Subject Leaders* (TTA 1998). Below is a list of skills and attributes mentioned in the document I consider relevant to *all* middle managers and the chapters in this book you will find relevant to each one.

	Skills and attributes	*Relevant chapters*
(a)	**Leadership skills – the ability to lead and manage people towards common goals.** Team leaders should be able to:	
1	secure commitment to a clear aim and direction for the subject	2, 3, 4, 6, 7, 9
2	prioritize, plan and organize	8, 9, 11
3	work as part of a team	5
4	deal sensitively with people, recognize individual needs and take account of these in securing a consistent team approach to raising achievement	4, 5
5	acknowledge and utilize the experience, expertise and contribution of others	2, 3, 4, 5
6	set standards and provide a role model for pupils and other staff	1, 4, 5
7	devolve responsibilities and delegate tasks, as appropriate	4, 9
8	seek advice and support when necessary	10, 11
9	command credibility through the discharge of their duties and use their expertise to influence others	4, 5, 6, 7

10	make informed use of research and inspection findings	3, 9, 10
(b)	**Decision-making skills – the ability to solve problems and make decisions.** Team leaders should be able to:	
1	judge when to make decisions, when to consult with others, and when to defer to senior managers	4, 5, 6, 7, 10
2	analyse, understand and interpret relevant information and data	9, 10
3	think creatively and imaginatively to anticipate and solve problems and identify opportunities	9
(c)	**Communication skills – the ability to make points clearly and understand the views of others.** Team leaders should be able to:	
1	communicate effectively, orally and in writing, with the head teacher, other staff, pupils, parents, governors, external agencies and the wider community	1, 6, 7
2	negotiate and consult effectively	4, 5, 6, 10
3	ensure good communication with, and between, staff in your team	6, 7, 9
4	chair meetings effectively	7
(d)	**Self-management – the ability to plan time effectively and to organize oneself well.** Team leaders should be able to:	
1	prioritize and manage their own time effectively	11
2	achieve challenging professional goals	4, 9, 10
3	take responsibility for their own professional development	1, 9, 10
(e)	**Attributes** Team leaders draw upon the attributes possessed and displayed by all successful and effective teachers in the context of their leadership and management roles including:	
1	personal impact and presence	1, 6, 7

2	adaptability	3, 5, 9
3	energy, vigour and perseverance	1, 4, 5
4	self-confidence	6, 7
5	enthusiasm	1, 2, 4
vi.	intellectual ability	10
vii.	reliability and integrity	1, 2, 3, 4
viii.	commitment	1, 9

References

Adair, J. (1997) *Leadership Skills.* London: IPD.

Ainscow, M. (1994) *Creating the Conditions for School Improvement.* London: David Fulton Publishers.

Belbin, R. M. (1981) *Management Teams: Why They Succeed or Fail.* London: Heinemann.

Belbin, R. M. (1993) *Team Roles at Work.* Oxford: Butterworth-Heinemann.

Blanchard, K. (1994) *Leadership and the One Minute Manager.* London: HarperCollins.

Bush, T. (1994) 'Theory and practice in educational management', in Bush, T. and West-Burnham, (eds), *The Principles of Educational Management.* Harlow: Longman.

Clarke, P. (1998) *Back from the Brink: transforming the Ridings School – and our children's education.* London: Metro Books.

Cooper, C. and Sutherland, V. (1997) *30 Minutes to Deal with Difficult People.* London: Kogan Page.

Cooper, M. (1998) *The Right Time to Sack a Poor Performer, TES,* 9 October 1998.

Covey, S. (1994) *First Things First: Coping with the ever increasing demands of the workplace.* London: Simon & Schuster.

Davies, B. and West-Burnham, J. (1997) *Reengineering and Total Quality in Schools.* London: Pitman.

DfE (1992) *Effective Management in Schools: A Report for the Department for Education via the School Management Task Force Professional Working Party.* London: HMSO.

DfEE (1998) *Teachers: Meeting the challenge of change.* London: DfEE.

Education Service Advisory Committee (1992) *Managing Occupational Stress: A Guide for Managers and Teachers in the School Sector.* London: HMSO.

Fontana, D. (1989) *Managing Stress.* London: Routledge.

Fullan, M. and Hargreaves, A. (1992) *What's Worth Fighting for in Your School?* Milton Keynes: Open University Press.

Giles, C. (1997) *School Development Planning: A practical guide to the strategic management process.* London: Northcote House.

Gold, A. and Evans, J. (1998) *Reflecting on School Management.* London: Falmer Press.

Hall, V. and Oldroyd, D. (1990) *Management Self-development for Staff in Secondary Schools, Unit 2: Policy, Planning and Change.* Bristol: NDCEMP.

Handy, C. and Aitken, R. (1986) *Understanding Schools as Organisations.* Harmondsworth: Penguin.

Hardingham, A. (1995) *Working in Teams.* London: IPD.

Hargreaves, D. and Hopkins, D. (1991) *The Empowered School: The management and practice of development planning.* London: Cassell.

Holly, P and Southworth, G. (1989) *The Developing School.* London: Falmer.

Hopkins, D. and MacGilchrist, B. (1998) 'Development planning for pupil achievement', *School Leadership and Management* **18**(3), 409–24.

Lewis, P. (1975) *Organisational Communications.* Colombus, Ohio: Grid.

MacGregor, D. (1960) *The Human Side of Enterprise.* Maidenhead: McGraw-Hill.

Maddux, R. B. (1986) *Team Building.* London: Kogan Page.

Marris, P. (1975) *Loss and Change.* London: Anchor Press.

Marsh, J. (1992) *The Quality Tool Kit: An A-Z of Tools and Techniques.* New York: IFS International.

Pacific Institute (1997) *Investment in Excellence: Personal Resource Manual.* Seattle: Pacific Institute.

Plant, R. (1987) *Managing Change and Making it Stick.* London: Fontana.

Riches, C. and Morgan, C. (1989) *Human Resource Management in Education.* Milton Keynes: Open University Press.

Sale, J. (1998) 'Keeping the dynamism: some basic tactics for avoiding stale meetings', *Managing Schools Today,* September 1998.

Sallis, J. (1997) 'Studies on change', *Managing Schools Today,* September 1997.

Sammons, P., Hillman, J. and Mortimore, P. (1995) *Key Characteristics of Effective Schools.* London: Institute of Education.

Sammons, P., Thomas, S. and Mortimore, P. (1997) *Forging Links: Effective Schools and Effective Departments.* London: Paul Chapman.

Smith, P. (1996) 'Tools for measuring quality improvement', *Management in Education* **10**(2), 5–7.

Teacher Training Agency (1998) *National Standards for Subject Leaders.* London: TTA.

Thomson, R. (1998) *People Management.* London: Orion.

Trethowan, D. M. (1991) *Managing With Appraisal.* London: Paul Chapman.

West, N. (1997) 'A framework for curriculum development, policy implementation and monitoring quality' in Preedy, M., Glatter, R., Levocic, R. (eds), *Educational Management.* Philadelphia: Open University Press.

Williams, E. (1999) 'Ofsteditis', *TES*, 26 March 1999.

Wood, I. (1991) *Time Management in Teaching.* London: NEP.

Index